C0-AUS-988

CHRIST

CHRIST

BY

VERY REV. W. R. MATTHEWS
K.C.V.O., D.D., D.Lit.

NEW YORK
THE MACMILLAN COMPANY
1939

First published 1939

Printed in Great Britain by Blackie & Son, Ltd., Glasgow

PREFACE

A SHORT book on the teaching of Jesus is open to two objections. On the one hand, it may be said that any such work is unnecessary, because we have the teaching of Jesus plainly set forth in the Gospels; on the other hand, it may be objected that so many complex questions are involved in the interpretation of the Gospels that no small book can be of much value. There is truth in both these contentions. Certainly the Gospels are, in the main, plain enough and any reader of ordinary intelligence and candour can gain from them a sufficient knowledge of what Jesus did and said. No one would be foolish enough to imagine that any book can take the place of the Gospels themselves. Equally true is it that a survey on the present scale must pass over many important topics to which a full discussion would give attention. But I hope that this book may be useful to some readers who wish to have guidance in studying the Gospels and who are perhaps perplexed by what they have heard of modern criticism of the New Testament. The purpose of the series in which the book appears is to state the teaching of the great men whose names stand on the title pages as objectively as possible, without criticism or advocacy, and as far as possible in their own words. I have tried to carry out this intention and to write in as detached a way as if I had been expounding the theories of Spinoza or Kant, but I can hardly believe that I have succeeded, for Jesus does not allow us to treat him as if he were merely a teacher. He challenges us to say what we think of him and not only what we think of his doctrine. One who shares the conviction of the authors of the Gospels that Jesus is the Son of God cannot write of him without betraying his belief. I believe, however, that I have given an honest account of what, in my opinion, any candid reader of the Gospels, whether believer or unbeliever, who was acquainted with modern research, would reasonably conclude to have been the doctrine of Jesus. To me, at least, the attempt to retain an attitude of complete objectivity has not had the effect of minimizing the impression which the person and words of Jesus make upon my mind and heart. I cannot think it will be otherwise with those who read.

I have to acknowledge obligations to many writers. To my old and revered teacher the Bishop of Gloucester and notably to his book, *The Life and Teaching of Jesus the Christ*, I owe very much—more perhaps than I could estimate. Dr. Streeter's great book, *The Four Gospels*, has been constantly before me, as it should be before every serious student. It will be seen that I have referred frequently to Dr. T. W. Manson's *Teaching of Jesus*, which is a book not only of great learning but also excellent judgment. The two small but extremely valuable books by Professor C. H. Dodd, *The Parables of the Kingdom* and *The Apostolic Preaching and its Developments* have influenced my thought greatly. The last book which Rudolf Otto wrote,

The Kingdom of God and the Son of Man, has the characteristics which marked his earlier work, *The Idea of the Holy*—immense learning, genius and the tendency to exaggerate one side of the truth at the expense of others. It is a book which leaves an indelible impression. I have constantly referred to the commentaries of Dr. Rawlinson on St. Mark and Professor Creed on St. Luke. In the use of capital letters I have followed the usage of the Revised Version of the New Testament.

CONTENTS

I

OUR SOURCES FOR THE KNOWLEDGE OF THE TEACHING OF JESUS

SO far as we know, Jesus of Nazareth wrote nothing and it is at least certain that no written words of his have come down to us. In this he resembles two other great teachers who, after him, have probably exercised a greater influence upon mankind than any others—the Buddha and Socrates. Jesus' teaching was probably entirely oral and we know of his utterances and thought ultimately through the effect which they produced on the minds of his disciples. It is necessary to keep this fact steadily in mind, because, on any view of his person, he was immeasurably greater than any of the "little flock" which gathered round him and, almost inevitably, his meaning was missed or not fully grasped. We know, in fact, that Jesus himself was painfully aware of the inadequacy of his followers to apprehend his insight. We have further to remember that the records on which we perforce rely for our knowledge of Jesus and his teaching were written in a different language from that which he used. Beyond any reasonable doubt, the Master spoke Aramaic, a Semitic tongue which had displaced Hebrew in Palestine as the speech of the people. The sayings of Jesus, as we find them in the Gospels, have been translated from the original language into another which is not Semitic and has a different structure. Some scholars, and in particular Dr. Torrey, believe that the Gospels were originally written in Aramaic, but this view is not generally accepted. In any case, however, the original material, whether it existed in the form of complete Gospels or detached written or oral traditions, has been transposed from Aramaic into Greek and we have to admit the possibility that mistranslation has obscured the primary meaning in some instances. One of the advances which have been made in New Testament scholarship in recent times is the recognition that it is important if possible to reconstruct the Aramaic text which lies behind the Greek. Nevertheless it must not be inferred from all this that any serious doubt exists about the main tenor of the teaching of Jesus. There is no good reason to doubt that, in by far the greater number of instances, the Greek has faithfully represented the meaning of the Aramaic.

For all practical purposes our knowledge of what Jesus taught is derived solely from the New Testament. This is not true without qualification, because there are some sources outside the Bible which give us some information, meagre and mostly of very doubtful authority, about what Jesus said. Dr. M. R. James has translated what remains of the literature concerning Christ which was current in some parts of the Church in the early centuries but which has not been included in the Christian Bible. Anyone who will take the trouble to read his *Apocryphal New*

Testament with his introductions will easily convince himself that little valuable tradition has been preserved in the "non-canonical" Gospels. That there may be other material still to be discovered was proved in a startling way by the publication in 1935 of *Fragments of an Unknown Gospel* from a Greek papyrus of the first half of the second century A.D.[1] which contains an apparently independent account of the healing of the leper and of sayings known to us from our Gospels, together with a few broken sentences to which no parallel can be found in the New Testament.

There is good reason to believe that sayings of Jesus which have not been included in the New Testament were known to the early Church, for we read in early Christian writers aphorisms attributed to the Lord which are absent from our Gospels. "Pray for the great and the little will be yours! pray for the earthly and the heavenly will come to you," is a saying recorded by Clement of Alexandria.[2] "Never be glad except when you look upon your brother in love," is quoted by St. Jerome from the Gospel of the Hebrews. Nor must we omit the strange sentences from the *Oxyrhynchus Papyri* (about A.D. 200): "Raise the stone and thou shalt find me, cleave the wood and I am there." "Let him that seeks cease not until he finds, and when he finds he shall be astonished, astonished he shall reach the Kingdom and having reached the Kingdom he shall rest."

But the most accessible evidence that there were

[1] *Fragments of an Unknown Gospel*, edited by H. Idris Bell and T. C. Skeat. (Published by British Museum Trustees.)

[2] Stromateis I, 24.

"floating" traditions current in the early Church which had not become incorporated with any continuous narrative is in the New Testament itself. In our English Bible the passage John vii. 53 to viii. 12 contains the story of the woman taken in adultery, with the memorable saying of Jesus, "Neither do I condemn thee, go and sin no more." This incident does not fit into the narrative of the Gospel of John at all naturally and differs from it in vocabulary and style. The fact that some manuscripts place it in the middle of the Gospel of Luke and others at the end of John confirms a suspicion, which is suggested by the passage itself, that it was a detached and independent story—a part of the "floating" tradition.

The sum of what may be collected from sources outside the New Testament is almost negligible. Apart from the evidence which it affords we should indeed have good reason for believing that a person named Jesus of Nazareth had existed and had been crucified under Pontius Pilate, that from him had originated a religious movement of great historical moment, but we should know little indeed of what he was and what he taught. The sources, however, are narrower still, for only in the Gospels do we find material for our estimate of the historical Jesus. It is surprising how little we learn from the rest of the New Testament about the life and words of Christ. Outside the Gospels only one saying is recorded: "It is more blessed to give than to receive." [1] We must not conclude from this that the Christians of the Apostolic age were indifferent to the facts of their Lord's life or that they

[1] Acts xx. 35.

were not acquainted with them. The absence of detailed references and quotations is due to the concentration of that creative generation of the Church upon the meaning of the death and resurrection of Jesus to the world.

How far are the four Gospels reliable historical records? We must answer this question before we can approach the subject of the teaching of Jesus. It should be remarked, at the outset of this enquiry, that the Gospels are not, and do not profess to be, the work of detached historians. If there are such beings as completely unbiassed historians (which may be doubted) the Evangelists are not among them. The Gospels come to us from the Christian Church; they are products of its life; they were written by men who believed that Jesus was the Messiah and Son of God; they are intended for the edification of the Christian community and as instruments of Christian propaganda. This does not mean that they are therefore unworthy of credence; the very importance which the authors attached to the person of Jesus would operate, not only as a spur to treasure all that could be learned of the words of the Master, but as a check upon reckless reporting of baseless fables and uncontrolled exercise of the imagination. We have to recognize, however, that the traditions may in some places have been coloured by the beliefs and circumstances of the early Church. Without any dishonesty and in perfect good faith the Evangelist, in some instances, may have given a turn to a saying of Jesus which made it applicable to some problem which was facing the Christian Church of the first century. Thus, for example, it is generally agreed by New Testament scholars that the interpretations of the Parables which are sometimes appended to them in the text of the Gospels do not necessarily represent what Jesus intended.

That the Gospel of St. Mark is the earliest of our four accounts of Jesus is as nearly certain as any conclusion on literary evidence can be. To have established the priority of Mark is one of the results of modern criticism which, in this matter, has reversed the common opinion of the Church that Mark abbreviated Matthew. The complete case for the priority of Mark cannot here be given, but we must notice the chief ground for believing this hypothesis to be true—that Mark is used by Matthew and Luke. Anyone who will read the first three Gospels (called "Synoptic" because they have a common view) must be struck by the fact that practically the whole of the material contained in Mark reappears in Matthew and Luke. In some cases there is almost identity of language while in others (e.g. the Sermon on the Mount) there is considerable divergence. Moreover, when Matthew and Luke differ from one another, it is found, in the vast majority of cases, that one of them agrees with Mark. No doubt other explanations can be conjectured for this phenomenon but none of them is so simple and satisfactory as that Mark was incorporated into the other two Gospels. The opening words of the Gospel of Luke tell us that "many had taken in hand to draw up a narrative concerning those matters which have been fulfilled among us"[1] and plainly

[1] Luke i, 1.

suggest that the author had made use of sources for his own work; one of those sources is before us in the New Testament—the Gospel of Mark.

If we now eliminate from Matthew and Luke all the material which seems to have come from Mark, we find that we have left still a great many verses which appear, in substance, in both Gospels. This fact has led to the further hypothesis that Matthew and Luke had another source, which no longer exists as a separate document. Scholars have given this source the name *Q* (German " Quelle ", a source). The reasons for believing that there is another source beside Mark which was used by Matthew and Luke are of the same character as those which convince us that both used Mark. They are not, in the main, of a technical character, and the plausibility of the hypothesis can be tested by every reader of the Gospels who will read Matthew and Luke side by side and ask himself what is the most reasonable explanation of their agreement in places where they are not using Mark. It should be added that some scholars do not believe that *Q* ever existed as a single independent document. To the present writer, however, the case for *Q* as a single source appears very strong.

When we have subtracted from Matthew and Luke all that belongs, according to our theory, to Mark and to *Q*, we still have some important material left—those passages which are " peculiar " either to Matthew or to Luke. It is clear that both the Evangelists incorporated other traditions which they derived from sources now impossible to identify. Some of the special material in Luke is of great value, including, as it does, the Parable of the Prodigal Son. It may be, of course, that this came from *Q* and for some reason was omitted by Matthew, though it is difficult to see what could have induced the Evangelist to leave out this masterpiece among Jesus' stories if he had it in his source. In the special material of Matthew and Luke we are able to see reflected their different points of view. Matthew has much more respect for the Jewish Law than Luke and includes sayings of Jesus which suggest that he came not to destroy the Law but to fulfil it and also his command to the Apostles to go neither to the Samaritans nor the Gentiles. Probably Matthew represents the standpoint of the Jewish Christian while Luke, who omits all such sayings, writes with the wider outlook of one who believed that " in Christ there is neither Jew nor Greek ".

This brief survey has made it clear that considerable importance attaches to the origin of the Gospel of Mark. There is a tradition which comes from the earliest days of the Church that Mark wrote down the teaching of Peter about Jesus. How far this tradition is to be trusted is a matter of acute controversy into which we cannot enter; it must, however, be asserted that there is evidence for it which may fairly be called " contemporary " with the Gospel itself,[1] for Papias, Bishop of Hieropolis in the first half of the second century, tells us that he knew a certain " elder " who had been a disciple of the Lord and who said that " Mark having become the interpreter of Peter, wrote

[1] Cf. Streeter, *The Four Gospels*, p. 17, and Lake, *Introduction to New Testament*, pp. 19, 20.

down accurately everything that he remembered, without however recording in order what was either said or done by Christ". Some perplexity is caused by the words "in order" in this passage, because the Gospel of Mark seems to give the best outline of the career of Jesus and to have more regard for chronological development than the others. It is possible that the word *taxis*, translated "in order", refers to the style and arrangement of the book and this would correspond with the character of Mark, which is the roughest and least literary of the Gospels. This tradition of a connexion with Peter is confirmed by two other early Christian writers, Clement of Alexandria and Irenaeus, who add that Mark wrote his Gospel in Rome, though they differ on the question whether it was written before or after the death of Peter. It would be difficult to set aside this early tradition, especially in view of the fact that no one would be likely to attribute the Gospel to such a comparatively unimportant person as Mark if he was seeking for some apostolic figure to give authority to the narrative. No one would have thought of Mark unless it was known that in fact he was the author.

To these considerations may be added one of a more "subjective" kind. The version of Christianity which is given to us in the speeches of Peter in the Acts of the Apostles and in the 1st Epistle of Peter is a simple one which shows few traces of the development of Christian teaching due to St. Paul. It consists mainly in the proclamation of the Messiahship of Jesus and that he is to judge the world, together with the need for repentance and faith in order to be saved. That something like this was the earliest Christian message is almost beyond question and the Gospel of Mark conforms very closely to this pattern. It is, so to speak, the account of the life of Jesus which fits in with and substantiates this message. For the Gospel of Mark is concerned primarily, not with the words, but with the works of Jesus, to show him as the Messiah, the Son of Man and Son of God, whose nature and mission were kept secret until the end and avowed openly only in the answer given by the Lord to the Sanhedrin, which led directly to his crucifixion.

The Apostle Peter was martyred under Nero after the great fire in Rome in A.D. 64. If we believe Irenaeus, who tells us that the Gospel was composed before the death of the great Apostle, we must assign its date as some time before A.D. 64; if we disbelieve him, the probable date would be A.D. 65 or 66. It needs no argument that the possession of a document which can claim, in the main, to represent the teaching of the most prominent of the original Apostles is a matter of supreme importance. We are here in contact with the report and impressions of one who had companied with Jesus in his "temptations" and had played a major part in the events which preceded and attended the rise of the Christian Church. It must, however, be conceded to those who doubt the truth of this very ancient tradition that there are certain features of St. Mark's Gospel which preclude us from holding that it reproduces the witness of Peter and nothing else. The passages Mark vi. 31–

vii. 37 and Mark viii. 1–ix. 1, seem to be two different accounts of the same events and it is probable that Mark has here drawn upon information from another source. Again it seems unlikely that Mark is right when he implies that the crucifixion took place on the day of the Passover and in this particular the Gospel of John is more probably correct. Nevertheless it remains true that a very strong case exists for believing that in the Gospel of Mark we have the substance of what Peter was accustomed to teach about the life and words of Jesus.

Concerning the other primary source, *Q*, much less can be said. As we have seen, its existence is a probable conjecture and we do not know what form it may have had as an independent document. It appears to have consisted almost entirely of discourses, though narrative was not wholly absent. Obviously it must have come into being some time before the composition of Matthew and Luke, since both used it, but the date of Matthew and Luke is uncertain. Papias informs us that Matthew wrote the Logia, or Oracles, of the Lord in Hebrew and it is not impossible that this refers to *Q*, but, in that case, it would seem that it must have been translated into Greek before it was used by the Evangelists. Some scholars have assigned a very early date to *Q* and would put it long before Mark in time, even perhaps tracing it to the lifetime of Jesus himself. There can be no definite conclusion on this matter, but to the present writer it appears evident that it must have been in existence before the year 70 A.D., the date of the destruction of Jerusalem.

In recent years the attempt has been made to go further in the analysis of the Gospels and the material out of which they are composed. " Form Criticism " is the name given to a method, employed by some scholars in Germany, America and England, by which it is hoped to penetrate behind the literary sources and gain some knowledge of the formation of the tradition on which they rest. The students of folk-lore have developed, for their purposes, a scheme for classifying stories according to their structure and it is suggested that a similar classification of the stories in the Gospels may throw light upon the circumstances in which they took their present form. How far this method is likely to help us to a further understanding of the Gospels is a matter of controversy. To the present writer it seems that so far little of value has been produced by the method in question beyond unverifiable conjectures, and it may be noted that two eminent critics, Professor Guignebert and Professor Kirsopp Lake, neither of whom could be suspected of any conservative bias, have little faith in the result of this type of criticism. Perhaps the wisest remark made upon this subject is that of the late Dr. Streeter who said: " If you are going to tell that kind of story that is the kind of way you would tell it." In fact it does not seem hopeful to imagine that the mere form of a narrative can tell us much about its origin.

We have so far said nothing about the fourth Gospel —that according to John. One of the most difficult and important preliminary questions which have to be answered is, how far we may draw upon this Gospel for information about the teaching of Jesus. The

Gospel of John is one of the spiritual classics of the world and one of the perennial sources of the deepest mystical Christian piety. No one who would understand the meaning of Christ for the world can afford to neglect this book, which is the production of a profound inspiration and insight. But unfortunately we cannot be equally certain of its value as a source for our knowledge of the historical Jesus.

The so-called " external " evidence for the Gospel is impressive enough. As it stands, the book claims to have been written by " the Disciple whom Jesus loved "[1] and an early tradition identifies him with John the Apostle, the son of Zebedee. Irenaeus, who was Bishop of Lyons at the end of the second century A.D., had been, when young, living at Ephesus and he tells us that, in his boyhood, he had heard Polycarp talk. (Polycarp was martyred in A.D. 155 at the age of ninety.) Polycarp said that he had known John the son of Zebedee in Ephesus. There is very little reason to doubt the Church tradition that John the Apostle lived in Ephesus up to an advanced age, and that he was a very young man at the time of the crucifixion.

The fact that perhaps the majority of New Testament scholars doubt the reliability of this tradition is due to the difficulty of supposing that the Gospel of John was written by an eye-witness. For this reason some are inclined to believe that it was written by another John, John the Presbyter, of whose existence there is some highly questionable evidence. The problem may be stated quite briefly: it consists in the difference between Mark and John in the picture

[1] John xxi

which they give of the life and teaching of Jesus. The problem does not arise only when we examine minute particulars; it is patent for any intelligent reader to discover. We have only to read rapidly through the Gospel of Mark and the Gospel of John in succession to be aware that we gain from the two books quite different impressions of the ministry of Jesus. It is unnecessary here to analyse the discrepancy in detail but attention must be drawn to some salient points. From Mark, supported by the other Synoptic Gospels, we should gather that the greater part of the ministry of Jesus took place in Galilee and was concluded by a very brief sojourn in Jerusalem before the crucifixion, but from John we should learn that Jesus made at least two visits to the capital. Far more important, however, is the divergence between the two Gospels on the subject of the claim of Jesus to be the Messiah. If we follow Mark, we are compelled to suppose that the Messiahship was kept secret from the people and, when the mystery was penetrated by Peter, the disciples were charged not to disclose it. In John, on the other hand, Jesus is represented as coming before the people from the first as the Son of God and the summons to the multitude is not, as in Mark, to enter the Kingdom of God but to believe in Christ. Again nothing can be more certain, if we accept the Synoptic Gospels as our guide, than that Jesus came proclaiming the Kingdom of God and that his teaching centred upon that conception; in the Fourth Gospel, however, there is almost no mention of the Kingdom and its place is taken by the idea of " eternal life " through faith in the Son of God. Further, Mark and John give us totally different accounts of the manner of the Lord's teaching. According to the Synoptic Gospels, Jesus made a constant and masterly use of parable and couched his religious and ethical doctrine in short epigrammatic and even paradoxical sayings; while, according to John, he used allegories, such as that of the vine and the branches, and expressed himself in long discourses in which it is not always easy to separate the words of the Master from the reflections of the Evangelist.

The difference in tone and contents between the Gospel of John and the other Gospels was commented upon in the early Church. Clement of Alexandria states that: "John, having observed that the bodily things had been exhibited in the Gospels, being exhorted by his friends, inspired by the Spirit, produced a spiritual Gospel." It is worthy of note that the words "bodily" and "spiritual" are sometimes used as equivalent to "literal" and "symbolical". Whether Clement meant this or not, we may take his word "spiritual" in both senses as a good description of the Fourth Gospel. It is, as we have remarked, the most mystical of all the New Testament writings and a treasury of the most far-reaching religious conceptions. It is also an interpretation of the life and person of Jesus as the author had come to know them through a long period of meditation and experience. Though it is of the highest value as a document which shows the development of Christian thought and a permanent possession of Christian devotion, it cannot be used as a primary source for the teaching of the historical Jesus. Very probably the purpose of the book included a desire to correct what seemed to the writer some dangerous tendencies of certain Christians at the time when he wrote; for example, an erroneous emphasis on the Second Coming of Christ and an opposite pseudo-" spiritual " belief that Christ had not really " come in the flesh ".[1] There is also probably an intention of correcting the Synoptic Gospels in places, notably on the question of the day of the crucifixion.

It would be an exaggeration to say that the Gospel of John is simply an allegory and that it has no historical basis. Evidently, however, it must be used with great reserve when we are attempting to give an account of the teaching of Jesus of Nazareth.

We may now sum up the results of this brief survey of our sources. In the Gospel of Mark we have an account of the life of Jesus which was composed about thirty years after the crucifixion. Its matter, however, comes from the earliest days of the Church for, written by a man who was closely associated with the Apostolic circle, it embodies, in substance, the teaching of Peter and thus links us directly with an original disciple of the Lord. In the additional matter which is common to the Gospels of Matthew and Luke we have two versions of a very ancient source which included much of the teaching of Jesus. In addition both Matthew and Luke preserve other traditions, some of which are, beyond reasonable question, authentic.

We must add a general consideration which supports the reliability of the Synoptic tradition as a whole.

[1] See an interesting discussion of this in Quick, *Doctrines of the Creed*, pp. 101 f.

The siege and complete destruction of Jerusalem in A.D. 70 marked a great change in the political, religious and social conditions of Palestine. After that terrible catastrophe the situation was rapidly transformed. The Gospels, in the main, represent what we know to have been the political and religious circumstances and ideas of the time preceding the fall of Jerusalem. Only by an almost inconceivable exercise of the historical imagination could later writers have reconstructed a vanished past with such fidelity. Though perhaps in Matthew and Luke there are traces of the influence of the experiences which attended the end of the Jewish state, the main body of the tradition is singularly free from such reflection backward of the catastrophe. Moreover Christian thought moved swiftly in the first generation. At the time when Mark wrote his Gospel St. Paul had finished his work of theological construction. It is an additional reason for believing in the general authenticity of the Synoptic tradition that it is so little affected by later Christian thought and practice.

The two extreme views then appear equally unreasonable. There is no good ground for the view that we know little or nothing of what Jesus taught and *a fortiori* there is no ground at all for the absurd idea that Jesus never existed. It is one of the curiosities of literature that there have been learned men who could read the Gospel of Mark and still hold that the central figure was a " sun myth ". But there is no good ground either for supposing that every saying attributed to Jesus in the New Testament comes from him without possibility of mistake or misinterpretation. If we would know what the historical Jesus taught, we must approach the question in a spirit of sane criticism. In the chapters that follow, we shall take for granted that Mark and *Q* are our most important authorities, without disregarding the special material of Matthew and Luke. We shall refer to the Gospel of John only when it seems to throw light on these fundamental texts.

II

JESUS AS TEACHER

IT is important to gain some clear conception of what kind of teacher Jesus was. There are two questions to be answered; what did he appear to the people who heard him to be? and in what way did he conceive himself? The answers to these two questions will not necessarily be the same, though one will throw light on the other.

A customary way of speaking of Jesus among those who have separated themselves from orthodox Christianity is to call Jesus a "Rabbi" and to suppose that he was perhaps the most enlightened and tolerant of those who bore the name. Now this conception of the character of Jesus and his teaching, whatever else may be said for it, has no support in our sources and is indeed contradicted by them. In the ordinary sense of the word, Jesus was certainly not a rabbi. The impression which he made upon the people was quite different: "He speaks with authority," they cried, "and not as the scribes." Jesus appeared to them to be not a rabbi but a prophet.

The distinction between these two types of teacher is fundamental and the perception that Jesus belonged to the latter category in the eyes of those who heard him is vital for an understanding of his words. It is well known that, at the time of the ministry of Jesus, the Jewish religion had become predominantly legalistic. When we use this word we do not necessarily imply that there was not a deeply spiritual religious value in the reverence for the Law of Moses which was the centre of Judaism. Recent studies of Judaism have taught us that, in some circles at least, a firm faith in God and a lofty moral ideal of life were fostered under the yoke of the Law. Judaism had, however, left its creative period behind, and lived on the inspiration of the past. For the orthodox Jew the will of God was disclosed in the Law of Moses and in the Prophets. The aim of the pious was so to regulate every action that all conformed to the Law of God. In order to do this it was necessary that the Mosaic Code should be applied to circumstances with which it did not explicitly deal. Whenever life is ordered by a code the need for its extension is certain to arise. Unforeseen conditions occur, the habits of life change, the social order is modified, and the Law as it stands provides no plain direction. When the law is believed to be the direct voice of God the expedient of adding to it is obviously out of the question. So there arises a system of interpretations and deductions by which the Law is stretched to cover the new requirements. This had happened in Judaism. "The tradition of the elders," which Jesus so severely criticized, was a body of decisions by learned men with the purpose of making the Law an effective instrument of regulation over the whole of life. Thus the Scribe was an important person. He was essentially an interpreter.

He spoke indeed with authority; he sat, as Jesus is reported by Matthew to have said, " in Moses' seat ", but he had a derived authority. His words had weight, because he could say: " Thus saith the Law."

Jesus, we are told, was occasionally addressed as " Rabbi " as a matter of courtesy, but he seems to have had no liking for the title and indeed forbade his followers to accept it for themselves. It is true that he is an interpreter of the Law and Prophets, but in a different manner from that of the Scribes. The spirit of the Law is his concern and, when asked for a summary of it, he quotes from the Old Testament the principles of love of God and love of the neighbour. Jesus belongs, however, to the long line of Hebrew prophets. Doubtless in the thoughts of his disciples, and in his own thought about himself, he was far more than a prophet, but we shall understand his method of teaching best if we conceive him as in the prophetic succession.

The Hebrew prophets are without any exact parallel elsewhere in the history of religion and it cannot be said that their consciousness is entirely comprehensible to us. They differ from one another in personal characteristics and in the nature of their message, but one thing they have in common, they speak in the name of the Lord. " The word of the Lord " comes to them and lays a compulsion upon them to utter the message. With authority and not as interpreters of a recognized code they cry: " Thus saith the Lord." The word which they have to speak is, almost invariably, contrary to the preconceptions of the orthodox and popular religion of their time.

They cast down the established order of worship; they deny the pleasant illusions of the patriotic, who believe that God will not allow his chosen people to be overthrown; and, above all, they proclaim that God is righteous and that his righteousness is manifested in judgment.

The mode in which Jesus spoke has obvious resemblances to the prophetic manner. The people were not wholly astray when they thought of him as "one of the prophets" and heard in his words the renewal of the prophetic utterance. We may observe, too, a resemblance to the career of the Old Testament prophets in the life of Jesus. The books of the prophets often record the great experience in which they were called to their high and dangerous office. Isaiah, Jeremiah, Ezekiel have left an account of the vision of God which was the beginning of their ministry, setting them apart as men who spoke in the name of Jehovah. The corresponding incident in the life of Jesus is the experience at his baptism by John the Baptist. According to Mark, who here evidently preserves the genuine tradition, it was an experience within the Spirit of Jesus and shared by no one else: "he saw the heavens rent asunder and the Spirit as a dove descending upon him: and a voice came out of the heavens, Thou art my beloved Son, in thee I am well pleased". This profound spiritual realization marks the beginning of Jesus' ministry and occupies the same place in his career as the vision in the Temple did in that of Isaiah.

But there are indications that, though the analogy of the prophets is illuminating, it is not sufficient.

That Jesus speaks with more even than the authority of the greatest prophet is manifest from the form of his declarations. He is not accustomed to use the phrase "Thus saith Jehovah" or to speak of "the word of the Lord" coming to him. The Scribe said: "Thus saith the Law"; the Prophet, "Thus saith the Lord"; Jesus says, "I say unto you". The implications of this mode of teaching are worth pondering and they would take us far if we pursued them, but it is sufficient here to connect them with the vision and the voice at Jordan. Here too the resemblance to the Prophets is accompanied by a striking difference. "Thou art my Son" is the word which Jesus heard, not "Thou art my servant or messenger". Adapting a phrase in the Epistle to the Hebrews, we may ask, to which of the Prophets said he at any time, Thou art my Son? This consciousness that he stood in a unique filial relationship with God is the source of that immediate and underived authority which characterizes the form of so many of Jesus' sayings.

The method of Jesus' teaching has, in one respect, a close resemblance to that of the Prophets. It is oracular and expressed in short, pithy sayings, which are often hard to interpret and were, in fact, often found difficult even by his close companions. The prophets were almost the antithesis of philosophers. They uttered the truth which they saw rather than conclusions which they had painfully reasoned out. It would not be true to say that there is no argument in the discussions of Jesus, but it is true that, for the most part, he states his doctrine, often in startling and paradoxical terms, and leaves it to germinate in the minds of his hearers. Matthew Arnold coined the phrase, " the sweet reasonableness of Jesus ". There could hardly be a worse description, for it suggests that he was a philosopher who appealed to the discursive intellect of his hearers, whereas, on the contrary, he spoke with authority, in challenging and disturbing sentences, to awaken faith and obedience, not curiosity.

Jesus was accustomed to speak to the crowds in parables—" without a parable spake he not unto them ". The word " parable " does not mean only a short story; it can be used for aphoristic and enigmatic sayings. We need not, therefore, suppose that Jesus spoke to the multitude only in the form of the parable in the English meaning of the term. Indeed our sources clearly indicate that he did not. But the parable, in the sense of the religious story, was a constant element in his public preaching. He did not invent the form. Something like it may be found in the prophets of the Old Testament. The prophet Nathan, reproving David for his guilt concerning Bathsheba, uses a parable with a direct application to the sin. Many of the vivid images and the symbolic actions of the writing prophets have a resemblance to the parable. The Jewish religious teachers of the time of Jesus had developed the art of conveying spiritual and moral matter by means of narrative. That Jesus was a master of this art and exercised it in a perfection never elsewhere attained needs no argument. Even from a literary point of view the Prodigal Son bears the marks of genius.

A problem arises, however, when we ask what was the purpose of teaching in parables. The obvious answer that they were intended to make spiritual truths clear to simple people does not fit the facts as the Gospels record them. At the conclusion of the parable of the Sower, Jesus cries, " Who hath ears to hear let him hear," and, in reply to " those that were about him with the twelve," when the crowd had gone he uses strange words, quoting from the call of Isaiah, " Unto you is given the mystery of the Kingdom of God; but unto them that are without all things are done in parables, that seeing they may see and not perceive and hearing they may hear and not understand, lest haply they should turn again and it should be forgiven them ".[1]

The plain meaning of these words, which is confirmed by the passage of Isaiah here quoted, is that the purpose of the parables, so far from being that of making clear the mystery of the Kingdom of God, was precisely the opposite—to conceal it. It may be, as some scholars think, that the Aramaic words which lie behind the Greek have been misunderstood and that the original meaning of " that " was not " in order that " but " so that ". If this were the case, the saying would describe the consequences of teaching in parables and not the purpose. And clearly it would be a violent paradox to assert that the only intention of the parables was to keep hidden the mystery of the Kingdom. If that were the aim, the obvious course would be complete silence. We have to account for the fact that Jesus spoke openly about the Kingdom of

[1] Mark iv. 9–12.

God but always in parables the meaning of which was withheld from the majority of his hearers.

A solution to the problem is found surely in the famous advice not to " cast pearls before swine ".[1] Holy things, supreme among which is " the mystery of the Kingdom ", are not to be disclosed indiscriminately to those who are not prepared for their reception. It is a grave misunderstanding of the ministry of Jesus to imagine that he wished to inaugurate a " mass movement " or that he had anything in common with the propagandist who by means of catch phrases and " slogans " bends crowds to his purposes which they do not grasp. The intention of the parables was, partly at least, not elucidatory, but selective. Jesus spoke in public words which gave a hint of the existence of the mystery of the Kingdom and an indication of its value for those " who had ears to hear ". For most, we cannot doubt, the parables remained striking utterances which were soon forgotten, but in some they aroused the thirst for fuller knowledge, and these were they who passed into the Kingdom, who " took it by force ", becoming members of that inner circle to whom was given to know the mystery.

We are thus led to notice a characteristic feature of the Lord's method of teaching which is often overlooked by readers of the Gospels. It had two aspects, that addressed to " those without ", to the " outsiders ", and that reserved for the circle of disciples. It is important to consider always when studying the words of Jesus to what audience they were addressed,

[1] Matthew vii. 6.

to the crowds, to enemies, or to disciples.[1] To the disciples he disclosed the meaning of the Kingdom and of his own place in it. But even this does not accurately state the facts as we gather them from Mark. Within the group which was specially attached to him Jesus did not speak openly from the first of all that was in his mind. This is clear from the way in which he dealt with the question of his own claim to be the Messiah. He allowed it to be discerned. At Caesarea Philippi he asked the disciples, "Who say ye that I am?" and Peter answered and said, "Thou art the Messiah".[2] It is evident that this confession of Peter's marks a turning-point in the ministry of Jesus and particularly in his dealing with the inner circle. Immediately after that momentous declaration we read that "he charged them that they should tell no man of him. And he began to teach them that the Son of man must suffer many things and be rejected by the elders and the chief priests and scribes and be killed, and after three days rise again".[3] That is to say, from this moment he began to impart the deepest mystery of the Kingdom, that the Messiah, the Son of man, must suffer and die.

It is worthy of notice that the fact that Jesus gave an esoteric teaching to his disciples may have some bearing on the problem of the Fourth Gospel. It is at least possible that the full account of the Master's discourses to the chosen band is not given in the Synoptic Gospels and that some of it is to be found in the Gospel of John.

[1] This point is worked out with great thoroughness in Manson's *Teaching of Jesus*. [2] Mark viii. 29. [3] Mark viii. 30, 31.

Before we close this chapter on Jesus as teacher it is necessary to remark that it may be most misleading to think of him primarily from that standpoint. Certainly it is not so that Mark represents him. He comes, not as the purveyor of new and true ideas, but as the proclaimer of a fact—that the Kingdom of God has drawn near. The opening of Jesus' public life is recounted in the following words: "After that John was delivered up Jesus came into Galilee preaching the Kingdom of God and saying, The time is fulfilled and the Kingdom of God has drawn near: repent and believe in the good news." Now the word translated "preaching" is that used of heralds, not of those who persuade but of those who proclaim.

III

THE FATHER

AT the root of the whole of the activity and teaching of Jesus is a conviction of the reality of God. " Conviction " is perhaps too weak a word to describe the sense of God's presence and power which we overhear, as it were, in his every word. Whether God exists and what is his nature are questions which have been discussed ever since man began to think about himself and his life in any coherent manner. The intellectual problem of the reality and character of the Divine is still the central concern of those philosophers who have not resigned themselves to a position of " learned ignorance ". There is no evidence that this age-long debate had any echo in the mind of Jesus. His recorded utterances contain no discussion of the reasons for belief in God; nor does he deal with the doubter. Probably no one among his audiences questioned the existence of God, but this absence of any comment on the possibility of scepticism must be interpreted as throwing light not only on the hearers but also on the consciousness of the Teacher. Jesus never wavered in his apprehension of the reality of the Father. He may have doubted about the will of God and found the purpose hard to read; but that there was a divine will and a Creator he never questioned.

The fatherhood of God has often been regarded as the central belief of Christianity and its distinctive contribution to religion. That this belief is a vital element in the Christian faith and that it has the authority of Jesus are beyond question. " Our Father who art in Heaven " is the beginning of the prayer which the Lord gave to his disciples as it is the beginning of Christian belief. In asserting, however, the fatherhood of God, Jesus was not uttering any original thought; nor would his phrase appear to any Jew as startling.

The idea of God as Father has had a long history and has taken many forms in the course of the development of religion. In the lowest stages of culture it appears as the myth that divine or supernatural beings are, in a literal sense, the progenitors of the tribe. When this crude conception has been left behind the Creator may be still spoken of as Father in a metaphorical sense, since He is the originator and " First Cause " of all existence.

The word " father ", however, may be used to indicate the character of God rather than his creative activity, and in the elaboration of this idea the Hebrews have played a notable part. Only among a people whose family life was strong and healthy could the epithet " Father " as applied to God be a source of high and noble conceptions of deity, just as it is notorious that to-day the decay of family life in some circles of modern society has weakened the appeal of the phrase " our Father " to those whose memories of home and parents are neither happy nor serene. That Jehovah stood in a special relation with the Hebrews, his chosen people, was a fundamental belief of Old Testament religion and is expressed in the idea of the covenant between God and the nation. This relation is due not to any merit on the part of the people but to the love of Jehovah for them. Hosea finds evidence of the paternal care of Jehovah for his people in the deliverance from Egypt—a constant theme of Hebrew devotion—" When Israel was a child then I loved him and called my son out of Egypt ".[1] In the later period of Hebrew religion, as reflected in the Old Testament, the individual takes the place which was formerly occupied by the nation and the fatherhood of God is naturally given an individual application. " Like as a father pitieth his children, so the Lord pitieth them that fear him."[2]

Of course, the two senses of the divine fatherhood—that of creative power and of tender care—do not exclude one another. The Hebrew never forgot the majesty and the overruling might of Jehovah. The two conceptions of fatherhood are united in such a passage as that of the later Isaiah: " But now, O Lord, thou art our father; we are the clay, and thou our potter; and we all are the work of thy hand. Be not wroth very sore, O Lord, neither remember iniquity for ever: behold, look, we beseech thee, we are all thy people."[3]

It is clear that when Jesus spoke of God as father he was adopting and developing an idea which was deeply entrenched in the religion of his people. Dr.

[1] Hosea xi, 1. [2] Psalm ciii. 13. [3] Isaiah lxiv. 8-9.

Manson has pointed out an interesting and perhaps significant fact relating to Jesus' use of the term " father " when speaking of God. In Mark all the cases where Jesus speaks in this manner occur after the confession of his Messiahship by Peter and none of them is found in sayings addressed to the people. An examination of *Q* seems to confirm this. If we may trust this evidence, it would appear that Jesus rarely spoke of God as father except to his disciples and to them only after the great turning-point in his ministry. Thus, so far as his public utterances are concerned, Jesus probably used the name of Father for God less than was customary with Jewish religious teachers. Dr. Manson explains this somewhat remarkable conclusion by the suggestion that the divine fatherhood was to Jesus so deep and intimate a spiritual experience that he spoke of it only to those who were, in some degree, prepared to understand it. To him it was no theological dogma, which was to be accepted as a belief, but a deep and present reality of experience.[1]

We have already referred to the unique " filial consciousness " of Jesus and emphasized its importance for any understanding of his teaching, but we must now refer to it again in connexion with the doctrine of the divine fatherhood. Evidently, from the first, those who came in contact with him felt that he was not as other men and those who were most closely attached to him came to recognize that even the idea that he was a prophet like one of the prophets of old was not adequate. This culminated in the decisive

[1] See *Teaching of Jesus*, Manson, pp. 108 f.

declaration of Peter: "Thou art the Messiah." That this perception of his transcendence of all categories corresponded with some consciousness of Jesus himself is left in no doubt by our Synoptic Gospels, and those critics who seek to reduce him to the stature of a Jewish rabbi can do so only by an arbitrary rejection of a great part of the evidence. We have the acceptance of the title of Messiah, about which more must be said later; we have the authoritative formula, "But I say unto you", contrasted with the prophetic, "Thus saith the Lord"; we have the voice heard by Jesus at the Baptism. To these we must add the absence of any indication that Jesus felt any sense of personal sin or separation from God. He, who called others to repent, shows no sign that he has needed repentance. A thanksgiving, reported from *Q* by Matthew and Luke, gives memorable expression to the consciousness which Jesus had of a unique relation with the Father. "I thank thee, Father, Lord of Heaven and earth, that thou hast hidden these things from the wise and prudent and hast revealed them to babes; yea, Father, for so it was well pleasing in thy sight. All things are delivered to me by my Father and no one knows the Father but the Son and he to whom the Son wills to reveal him." This is immediately followed by the invitation, "Take my yoke upon you and learn of me".[1] This passage is naturally not regarded as a genuine saying of Jesus by those critics whose theory requires them to deny every indication that Jesus was above the stature of ordinary humanity. We can only say that there is no ground in the manuscripts

[1] Matthew xi. 25–27. Luke x. 21–22.

for rejecting it, and that it stands in one of our primary sources. The only evidence we have is of one who was recognized by himself and by his intimate companions as standing in a relation with God which no other human being occupied. If our philosophy, or our prejudice, forbids us to believe that such a person could exist, we can doubtless find plausible explanations of how the belief that he existed could have grown up, but let us not pretend that our conjectures are history or that they are supported by the documents.

The Hebrew and Jewish conception of God was entirely concrete and religious. The philosophical idea of the ultimate principle of being has little or no place in the Old Testament doctrine of God. To the Prophets Jehovah is, before all things, the living God, a personal being of unlimited power and wisdom. Thus the assertion that God has a will and purpose, which has caused much debate in the schools, would seem to the Jew no paradox but a necessary and obvious corollary to the belief that God exists. It was the special privilege and function of the prophet to know and declare the will of God for his generation and it was the supreme duty and blessedness of men to obey that will. To the Jew of our Lord's day the will of God had been revealed finally and sufficiently in the Law and the Prophets. Jesus accepts to the full the Jewish faith in God as personal and living, and also the consequence that God has a purpose to be done. Thus he teaches the disciples to pray "Thy will be done as in heaven so on earth"; and in his own agony of mind in the Garden of Gethsemane, when he prays that the cup of sacrifice may pass from him, he adds, " Not as I will but as thou wilt ".

Jesus then taught that God is the personal creative life and that he can be described as a Father whose will and purpose for men is loving beyond the measure of any human fatherhood. In connexion with this aspect of his teaching we have some indication of the manner in which his thought moved. It has some resemblance to a method employed in philosophical theology and named the " Via Eminentiae ", according to which all " perfections " or " values " which we find in the created order may be ascribed to God, only in the " most eminent degree ", i.e. with all limitations removed. So Jesus says, " If ye then, being evil, know how to give good gifts to your children, how much more will the Father give the Holy Spirit (or ' good things ' Mat.) to those who ask him ".[1]

That the mercy as well as the will of God is over all his works is the deep conviction of Jesus. Not a sparrow falls to the ground without the Father. There is no sphere or aspect of existence which is outside the loving care of God. Professor Dodd, in his notable book on the Parables of the Kingdom, has pointed out that the presupposition on which they are based is that the natural and supernatural orders have an affinity with one another, they are in fact one order, and consequently it is possible to " take any part of that order and find in it illumination for other parts ". " This sense of the divineness of the natural order is the major premise of all the parables." [2] No one can

[1] Matthew vii. 11. Luke xi. 13.

[2] *Parables of the Kingdom*, Dodd, p. 22.

read the Gospels without being aware that Jesus looked upon nature with the eye of a poet and artist. He had a joy in natural things and in the common processes of seed-time and harvest as well as in the simple lives of common people. But this was not a merely aesthetic pleasure. To him these scenes and mo[illegible]ents spoke of God, to him all nature and human l[illegible]as permeated by the divine life and manifested [illegible] Father's loving will.

This belief in God, which was central in the teaching of Jesus, has consequences of a practical kind in the life of the individual. It is the ground of that morality of the motive and the heart which is the theme of the Sermon on the Mount. The Father " sees in secret ", his vision penetrates to the inner desire and impulse from which action springs. Hence Jesus carries forward the highest insight of the greater prophets that righteousness does not consist in the conformity of the outward conduct to a rule but in the " humble and contrite spirit ". A man cannot be right with the God who " searcheth the very heart and reins " unless he is renewed in the inner man.

The realization of the fatherhood of God is the sovereign remedy for what Jesus recognized as a terrible spiritual disease—anxiety. The son of the Kingdom is not told, as unfortunately our Authorized Version has misled many into believing, to " take no thought " for the morrow, but he is most emphatically told not to be anxious what he shall eat or drink or wear. The lilies of the field are clothed by the Father and the birds are fed. He knows the needs of his children. And the burden of care which oppresses the majority of the human race will be lifted if we really believe in God, for then we shall be seeking first of all his Kingdom and his righteousness. Nor will the fear of the power and injustice of men be a source of crippling anxiety to the believer. Terror of those who can kill the body and then have nothing more that they can do will be swallowed up in awe of him in whose power is the soul itself and its eternal destiny. Thus the man who believes in God, as Jesus understood believing, is armed against all deprivations, adversities and alarms. " It is not the will of the Father that one of these little ones should perish." Anxiety is abolished. " Fear not, little flock, for it is your Father's good pleasure to give you the Kingdom."

IV

THE KINGDOM OF GOD

WE read in Mark, as the first words of the narrative which that Gospel gives of the public ministry of Jesus: "Now after that John was delivered up Jesus came into Galilee proclaiming the good news of God and saying, The time is fulfilled and the Kingdom of God is at hand (or has drawn near), repent and believe in the good news." Thus the note is struck which dominates the whole of the life and teaching of Christ. There can be no doubt that the Kingdom of God was the theme which ran through the whole, and therefore, if we would grasp the meaning of the doctrine as a unity, we must make an effort to understand what Jesus conceived the Kingdom to be. The words of Mark indicate also that the vision of Jesus was, in some sense, a continuation of that of John the Baptist, or at least that the careers of the two prophets, as they seemed to the populace, were understood to be closely related. Unfortunately the evidence of our authorities on the subject is not conclusive and we cannot say with certainty whether John also announced the coming of the Kingdom of God. Mark tells us simply that he baptised in the wilderness and preached a baptism of repentance for the forgiveness of sins. Luke adds that he warned his hearers to flee from the wrath to come, and both agree that he looked forward to the appearance of "one mightier" than he. John does not agree with the Synoptic Gospels in thinking that the public ministry of Jesus began only after John's imprisonment and is obviously anxious to underline "the witness of John" to the Lord; thus the Fourth Gospel represents him as testifying that in the midst of his audience stood "one whom they knew not"—the one who was to come. Only in Matthew is the burden of John's message said to have been the Kingdom and he uses precisely the same words to describe the message of John as those in which he summarizes the message of Jesus. Since elsewhere Matthew seems to attribute words to John which really were those of Jesus his evidence here is open to question. It is probably safer to trust the impression which we gain from Mark and suppose that the Kingdom did not occupy a prominent place in the teaching of John. In any case, it is evident that, from the first, the preaching of Jesus was felt to be something fresh—"a new doctrine".

The meaning of the Kingdom of God may justly be said to be the most burning question in Christian theology at the present time. It affects not only the interpretation of the New Testament and the life of Christ but the whole problem of Christian action in the world to-day. This was plainly shown in the Oxford Conference of Christian Churches in 1937, where Church, Community and State was the subject of discussion. It was evident there that two conceptions of the function of the Church were present, which sprang from two conceptions of the nature of the Kingdom of which the Church is the instrument. There were those who held that the Church's task is to co-operate in the work of civilization and to be its soul and inspiration, while others believed, on the contrary, that the Church has only an accidental relation with secular society and that its function is mainly to save men out of this present world, which is fundamentally and in principle hostile to God. Both in the sphere of New Testament study and in that of Christian theology there has been a reaction against the theory, so popular in the years before the War, that the Kingdom of God could be equated with social progress or with the realization of a condition of human society which embodied the two great principles of the fatherhood of God and the brotherhood of man.

The phrase "Kingdom of God" in English is misleading, because it suggests a community or realm over which God reigns. The idea, however, which is conveyed by the Aramaic words which have been thus translated is primarily that of the ruling, the sovereignty, the active exercise of kingly power—the act rather than the object of the act. The thought that Jehovah reigns over his people is one of the most obvious and persistent in the Old Testament. Kingship in many religions has been invested with a divine character and in the early ritual and myth of Semitic peoples it seems that the figure of the divine king, or the king who was also a god, played a prominent part. But the idea that Jehovah was the true king of Israel appears to have retarded the development of the monarchy among the Hebrews. Gideon refused to accept the office, on the ground that Jehovah is the king. One of the two accounts which have been combined in 1st Samuel evidently represents the view of those who regarded the appointment of Saul as king as an act of rebellion against the kingship of Jehovah. Another line of thought, however, was destined to prevail—that of the divinely inspired king. This conception of a king who should rule in righteousness and bring peace and prosperity to his people is the germ of the figure of the Messiah and of the Kingdom of the Messiah which is of such decisive importance in the development of Jewish and Christian thought. Men looked back upon the great days of David, which doubtless were idealized by later generations, and imagined a return of that golden age, only yet more glorious, and a king of the house of David greater than he.

Associated with this hope of the Messianic Kingdom was the idea of " the Day of the Lord ". The original thought was simply that of a great day of national deliverance on which the Lord of Hosts, the God of the Armies of Israel, would overthrow all Israel's enemies and execute judgment and vengeance upon them. In the hands of the Prophets these ideas became transformed. The Kingdom of God ceased to be merely a dream of nationalist triumph and revenge and was given a deeply moral and spiritual connotation, until at last, in the writings of the nameless prophet whose remains are incorporated in the book of Isaiah, the future triumph is a spread of the knowledge of God that the Hebrews possessed throughout the whole earth, and something like a league of nations, bound together by a common worship and having its spiritual centre at Jerusalem, is depicted. It should be observed that the idea of the reign of God does not necessarily involve the idea of the Messiah and, in fact, he does not appear in some of the prophets.

The conception of a divine judgment, which is implicit in the hope of a Day of Jehovah, also underwent a process of development. The crude imagination of a slaughter of enemies was replaced by the image of a judgment upon all peoples which would " begin with the House of Israel ". The earliest of the writing prophets, Amos, protests against the easy optimism with which those who themselves deserved the divine wrath looked forward to God's day. " Woe unto you," he cries, " that desire the day of the Lord! Wherefore would ye have the day of the Lord? It is darkness and not light; as if a man did flee from a lion and a bear met him; or went into the house and leaned his hand on the wall, and a serpent bit him." [1] This belief that God's judgment will usher in God's reign is deeply impressed upon the Hebrew religious consciousness; doubtless it was this theme of ancient prophecy which John the Baptist revived when he called men to flee from the wrath to come by repentance.

We must remember that this complex of religious beliefs and images, which we have briefly sketched, was in the mind both of Jesus and his hearers. Every word of his presupposes it. It is the " universe of discourse " within which his own thought and that of

[1] Amos v. 18–19.

the multitudes moved. The best preparation for understanding the New Testament, indeed the indispensable preliminary, is an intelligent knowledge of the Old.

We have now to mention a complex of religious thoughts and images which, though closely related with those which we have just discussed, are in some important respects different. The Apocalyptic literature and its relevance for the interpretation of the teaching of Jesus is an intricate subject on which we must be content to speak in the most general terms. It is unfortunately mixed up with topics on which there are unsettled controversies and it must be stated that some scholars would question the value of this literature for the understanding of the New Testament. The main body of opinion, however, is on the side of those who believe that we have much to learn from these writings. The word " Apocalypse " means literally " unveiling " and the name is given to certain books because they profess to draw the veil from the future and reveal the secrets of divine providence. Though many Apocalyptic writings have come to our knowledge only recently, the existence of this type of book and the attitude which it represents have always been known, because we have two examples in the Bible—the Book of Daniel and the Revelation of St. John. The documents of this movement are of various dates, ranging from 200 B.C. to A.D. 100, and the authors are all anonymous, hiding their identity under some great name from the past such as Enoch and the Patriarchs.

The Apocalyptic writings are the product of a

period when the Jewish dream of a great deliverance had suffered a final disillusionment. After a glorious but brief spell of independence under the Maccabees the Jewish state had once more become a vassal of the great world powers and finally a part of the Roman Empire. In these circumstances the unquenchable hope and faith of Judaism took a more pronounced other-worldly form. Whereas the Prophets had looked for the judgment of God and His reign within history, the Apocalyptic thinkers held a more drastically pessimistic view of the present world. The reign of God would not come in history in the ordinary sense of that word. It must be through a divine action which would bring the process of the present age to a stop and inaugurate the New Age in a new heaven and a new earth. It would be a mistake to suppose that these books present us with a fixed and coherent system of ideas. Their pictures are often vague and floating like dream imagery. Certain themes, however, make a constant appearance: the idea of judgment and the relegation of the wicked Jews and the heathen to Sheol: the idea of resurrection from the dead: the idea that the day of the Lord will be preceded by great tribulations, wars and convulsions of nature. The doctrine of angelic beings, good and evil, is developed in these writings far beyond the position of the Old Testament and the important religious conception of a conflict between the organized powers of evil and those of good, together with the belief in an ultimate triumph of God, plays a considerable part.

It should be observed that we do not know how

far this complex of ideas and images was accepted by the mass of the people in Palestine in the time of Jesus. It may be that they were current only in a comparatively small circle or, on the contrary, they may have been widely spread. It is certain that, in the long run, the religion of orthodox Jews rejected the Apocalyptic literature and outlook.[1]

Having now reviewed some of the conceptions of the Kingdom which were current at the time when Jesus taught, we must attempt to sum up his doctrine and see how far he accepted them and how far he transformed them. In dealing shortly with the subject it is necessary to be dogmatic if we are not to lose ourselves in the details of the discussion. To the present writer it seems clear that, in the cautious words of Professor Dodd, Jesus had " on some sides much sympathy with the ideas of the Jewish Apocalyptists ", but the theory that he accepted them without profound modification is not in accordance with our evidence. The important point to notice is that, in the teaching of Jesus, the Kingdom of God has a twofold aspect. On the one hand, it has come, it is a present fact; on the other, it will come " in power " hereafter. We cannot make any coherent sense of the sayings of Jesus on this subject unless we keep firmly in mind that for him the Kingdom is both a present reality and a future promise.

Some of the most familiar words of Jesus presuppose that the Kingdom of God is already there. It must be accepted now. Whoever does not receive it as a little child will never enter it.[2] It is a matter of

[1] See Oesterley, *The Books of the Apocrypha*, p. 199. [2] Mark x. 15.

experience to those who are with Jesus. They are participators in the events of the "fullness of times". "Blessed are the eyes which see the things that ye see, for I say unto you that many prophets and kings desired to see the things which ye see and saw them not and to hear the things which ye hear and heard them not."[1] Again, Jesus pictures the Queen of Sheba and the men of Nineveh rising in judgment against the men of his own generation because a "greater than Solomon" and a "greater than Jonah" was among them. When Jesus sent out the seventy missionaries "as lambs in the midst of wolves" he enjoined them to say both to those who received and those who repelled them, "The Kingdom of God has come near to you:" which means not, Prepare for the Kingdom which will come very soon, but, The opportunity of entering the Kingdom, which is here and now, has been presented to you. St. Luke tells us that, being asked by the Pharisees, when the Kingdom of God comes, he answered, "The Kingdom comes not with observation: neither shall they say, lo here, or lo there, for the Kingdom of God is in your midst".[2] There can be no doubt that the significance of all these passages and others is that, with Jesus, the Kingdom had come already: the new age of the reign of God had begun.

But we should misinterpret the meaning of this if we supposed that it implied simply that a new and purer conception of God had been introduced into the world or even that one had come who was in complete and unbroken communion with the Father.

[1] Luke x. 23, 24. [2] Luke xvii. 20, 21.

Jesus is in agreement with the Prophets and the Apocalyptists when he speaks of the Kingdom as the manifestation of the creative and redeeming power of the Father. It is not so much a new doctrine as a new divine energy in the world to which Jesus points as the sign of the present Kingdom. This is plain enough in the answer which he gave to the messengers from John the Baptist, who had doubted whether after all Jesus was He that was to come. "The blind receive their sight and the lame walk, the lepers are cleansed and the deaf hear, and the dead are raised up, and the poor have good tidings preached to them. And blessed is he whosoever shall find none occasion of stumbling in me."[1] These words have a reference to the pictures of the future "good time" in the Prophets, and their whole point is to suggest that the presence of the Kingdom is shown by the working of the divine power through and in the ministry of Jesus. Both Matthew and Luke tell us that this incident was followed by a comment on the place of John the Baptist in the providential order. He was "a prophet and more than a prophet", because he stood on the threshold of the Kingdom, "but he that is little in the Kingdom of Heaven is greater than he." "All the prophets and the law prophesied until John," "from that time the good news of the Kingdom is proclaimed and every man entereth forcibly into it."[2] The career of John marked the end of the preparation, the Law and the Prophets: from the advent of Jesus begins the new age of the Kingdom.

That this is the teaching of Jesus is confirmed by

[1] Matthew xi. 5, 6. Luke vii. 22, 23. [2] Luke xvi. 16.

the demands which Jesus makes of his disciples. Because with him the Kingdom of God has come, a man must love him more than father or mother, son or daughter and take up his cross and follow.[1] He who confesses Jesus before men will be confessed by the Son of Man before the angels of God and he who denies Jesus will be denied by the Son of Man.[2]

Beyond reasonable doubt Jesus required a devotion and service to himself on the part of his followers which can only be explained by the consciousness that he stood in such an unprecedented relation with the Father that service of Him was service of the Kingdom.

We cannot pass over without comment a feature in the evidence which gives rise to a difficult problem for modern Christians. One of the significant signs of the actual existence of the Kingdom is the conquest of demons. " If I by the finger of God cast out demons then is the Kingdom of God come upon you." [3] As we have seen, the myth of a conflict between organized spiritual powers of good and evil is an element in the Apocalyptic outlook. This conception is reflected in the words of Jesus. In refuting the charge that he cast out demons " by Beelzebub " he asks, " How can Satan cast out Satan?" and adds " if a Kingdom be divided against itself it cannot stand ". According to Luke, when the seventy missionaries " returned with joy saying Lord, even the demons are subject unto us in thy name," he replied: " I beheld Satan fallen as lightning from heaven. Behold I have given you authority to tread upon serpents and scorpions and

[1] Matthew x. 37. [2] Luke xii. 8, 9. [3] Luke xi. 20. Matthew xii. 28.

over all the power of the enemy, and nothing shall in any wise hurt you. Howbeit in this rejoice not, that the spirits are subject unto you, but rejoice that your names are written in heaven."[1] There can be no doubt that the tradition attributes to Jesus the belief that demons were the cause of bodily and mental disease and that his healing power is represented as a sign of the victory of the Kingdom of God over the forces of evil. Perhaps we cannot be certain that Jesus shared this belief, but at least there is no record of any saying of his that calls it in question.

We have seen that the Kingdom of God is announced by Jesus as a present fact and that it has come into the world, not as an idea which may spread nor as an ideal which may ultimately prevail, but as a breaking forth in Jesus himself of the divine power. We must now observe that there are sayings of Jesus which seem to indicate that the Kingdom does, in some sense, develop and enlarge. The chief passages with this implication are the so-called "Parables of Growth", the seed growing secretly and the leaven which leavens the whole lump. The meaning of these stories seems to lie on the surface and probably few readers would have any hesitation in assuming that the idea conveyed is that of the gradual extension of the Kingdom in the world. We must, however, admit that many competent interpreters reject this meaning and find the essence of these parables in the suddenness of the growth, surpassing reasonable expectations, or in the fact that the process is independent of the work of man. Probably this latter idea is present.

[1] Luke x. 17–20.

The Kingdom of God is, as Otto puts it in a memorable epigram, "God's seed not man's deed." But it is difficult to believe that the verdict of common sense is not right and we may venture to hold that illustrations drawn from growing things are intended to express the idea of growth.

We owe an interesting suggestion to Dr. Manson which has a bearing on this matter. He believes that a change in the Lord's manner of speaking of the Kingdom can be discerned when we compare his sayings before the confession of the Messiahship by Peter with those that belong to the period subsequent to that event. In the later part of his ministry Jesus speaks of entering the Kingdom, whereas in the earlier part he speaks rather of its coming. Though perhaps we ought not to lay too much stress on this, at least the hypothesis is attractive that Jesus saw in the recognition of his own divinely appointed place in the Kingdom the beginning of its coming in the world, the first stage of the growth by which the seed was to become a tree of life.

V

THE KINGDOM OF GOD AND THE SON OF MAN

THE reader may remember that in the last chapter we stated that, in the teaching of Jesus, the Kingdom of God had two aspects—a present and a future. We have now to discuss the idea of the Kingdom as a future promise, but, in order to do so, we must first deal with the meaning of the term " Son of Man ". This is necessary because many of the most important sayings which refer to the coming of the Kingdom refer also to the figure of the Son of Man.

According to the tradition preserved in the Synoptic Gospels, Jesus called himself and referred to himself as the Son of Man. What did this title imply? The actual phrase " Son of Man " is the literal translation of two Aramaic words which mean simply " the Man ". There are passages in the teaching of Jesus where " Son of Man " may most naturally be taken as equivalent to " Man ". Thus in the famous dictum about the Sabbath, " The Sabbath was made for man and not man for the Sabbath; the Son of Man is therefore lord also of the Sabbath ", it may be argued that the sense requires nothing more than " Man is lord of the sabbath ". But in the majority of cases where the phrase occurs it is evidently intended to be a personal title, and we are meant to gather that Jesus was "the Man", or the Son of Man, in a sense which is not applicable to other men. Thus when Jesus says, "The foxes have holes and the birds of the air have nests, but the Son of Man hath not where to lay his head", he plainly means that he, unlike other men, is homeless.

"The Son of Man" is a phrase with a history. We meet it, or rather something like it, in Ezekiel where the prophet is commanded by Jehovah, "Son of Man stand upon thy feet and I will speak to thee". Again in the book of Daniel we read of "one like unto a Son of Man".[1] The phrase occurs in a symbolical vision in which the prophet depicts the world empires which have dominion in succession over the earth. The cruel tyrannies of heathen powers are represented under the form of beasts; the fourth and last empire, that of "the people of the saints of the Most High", is symbolized as "one like unto a Son of Man", i.e. humane as contrasted with bestial. Here the phrase is almost certainly not the name of any personal being: the imagery is purely symbolical. In the Book of Enoch, however, one of the most important of the Apocalyptic writings, we meet the exact phrase employed in the Gospels: "the Son of Man". Here the figure is no mere symbol but a personal, supernatural being. He is the Messiah, a pre-existent person who is to judge all creatures and introduce the new age, banishing the unrighteous Jews and all heathen to "the flame of the pain of

[1] Daniel vii. 13.

Sheol ". The righteous Jews will inhabit a new heaven and a new earth.

Though the question is still controversial, there can be little doubt that Jesus identified himself with the Son of Man and that, in doing so, he had in mind the passage in Daniel and also, most probably, the Book of Enoch. In Dr. Otto's careful phrase, " Jesus let it be known and not only to his more intimate disciples that in his activity he was the personal representative of that Son of Man." " Every one that shall confess me before men him also shall the Son of Man confess before the angels of God." [1] When he began to speak of his approaching suffering he said, " The Son of Man must suffer many things and be rejected ". Only twice did Jesus break the silence which he maintained before his judges. To Pilate's question, " Art thou the King of the Jews?" he replied, " Thou sayest," claiming to be the Messianic King. When the High Priest asked, " Art thou the Messiah, the Son of the Blessed?" he replied, " I am; and ye shall see the Son of Man sitting at the right hand of power and coming with the clouds of heaven ", with an obvious reference to the seventh chapter of Daniel.

We may conclude that Jesus identified himself with the Son of Man, that in his thought it was a Messianic title and that it was connected with the future coming of the Kingdom in power.

If we now try to gather together the teaching of Jesus about the future Kingdom of God we are confronted with several difficulties and possible mis-

[1] Otto, *The Kingdom of God and the Son of Man*, p. 227.

understandings. It is vital to avoid the misconception that the present Kingdom is different from the future Kingdom. The Kingdom which came with Jesus is the same Kingdom as that which, at the end, will come with glory. Those who enter the Kingdom now have already become partakers of the powers of the coming age. This was an element in the teaching of Jesus which was faithfully preserved by the Apostolic Church when it regarded itself as an outpost of the Kingdom in the age which was already passing away.

The chief difficulty which arises about the teaching of Jesus concerning the Kingdom as coming arises from an apparent discrepancy between different sayings. In Mark xiii we have a long discourse delivered by Jesus, as he sat on the mount of Olives, in answer to the question of Peter, James, John and Andrew, " When shall these things be? and what shall be the sign when these things are all about to be accomplished?" The long reply is so full of Apocalyptic imagery that it has been called " the little Apocalypse " and, in the opinion of many scholars, once existed as a separate document. Many would regard it as not a genuine utterance of Jesus. It may be suspected that the motive for this doubt is the inconvenience which this passage causes to certain theories about the teaching of Christ. There is at least no ground in the manuscripts for excising it from our Gospels and we must observe that it appears, in a somewhat elaborated form, in both Matthew and Luke. Jesus here describes the " woes " which must precede the coming of the Kingdom, some of which appear to refer to the calamities which attended the siege of Jerusalem in A.D. 70.

The suggestion here is of an extended period before the end, of a time when the followers of Jesus will be persecuted, and it is definitely stated that the gospel must first be preached unto all the nations.[1]

The picture which is here given of the troubles which will be the signs of the approach of the Kingdom and of the intervening period is not easy to reconcile with other sayings of Jesus even in this same chapter, for he adds, "Verily I say unto you this generation shall not pass away until all these things be accomplished". There is, however, in this strange discourse a saying which is of primary importance. "Of that day or that hour knoweth no one, not even the angels in heaven, neither the Son but the Father."[2] The short answer to the question, When did Jesus think the Kingdom would come in its full glory? is that he said he did not know. Some critics have doubted whether he can have said this, but it may be pointed out that the Church is very unlikely to have invented a saying which attributed a limitation to the knowledge of the Lord.

We must bear this declaration of ignorance in mind when we consider other sayings which have a different tendency. There are words which certainly imply that Jesus expected the end very soon. "Verily I say unto you there be some of them that stand here which shall in no wise taste of death until they see the Kingdom of God come with power."[3] Jesus addresses urgent warning to his hearers to watch and pray because they do not know the hour. The day will come like a thief in the night when no one is

[1] Mark xiii. 9, 10. [2] Mark xiii. 32. [3] Mark ix. 1.

looking for it. These utterances strongly suggest that Jesus expected the coming within the lifetime of those who heard him.

What were the exact words which he spoke at his trial before the Sanhedrin? If we accept Mark's account, he said to those who were then present, "Ye shall see the Son of Man coming with the clouds of heaven", intimating that before they died they would be confronted with the Day of Jehovah and the Son of Man. Matthew and Luke give different versions, both of which introduce the word "henceforth". "From henceforth shall the Son of Man be seated at the right hand of the power of God."[1] "Henceforth ye shall see the Son of Man sitting at the right hand of power."[2] Evidently the effect of this modification is to remove the explicit prophecy of a definite event and to suggest a continuous process or the attainment of a permanent status from the time of the passion. Luke's text clearly makes the words of Jesus an anticipation of the Ascension, which he alone among the Evangelists records. It is impossible to be certain on this point, but the balance of probability is in favour of Mark's account, since it is easier to see how the words in his narrative could have been slightly changed, to avoid what seemed in later years a prediction which had not been fulfilled, than to see how the words as given by Matthew or Luke could have given rise to Mark's challenging sentence.

As we have seen, both the Prophets and the Apocalyptic writers connect the coming reign of God with a judgment. The "Day of the Lord", which begins

[1] Luke xxii. 69. [2] Matthew xxvi. 64.

the new age, is a day of retribution and separation of the just from the unjust. This element is clearly present in the teaching of Jesus about the Last Things. There are, however, remarkable differences between the manner in which the final judgment is conceived by Christ and the view of the Apocalyptic books. An unpleasant feature of many of these pictures is the indiscriminate condemnation of all the heathen. Jesus, on the contrary, attributes no special privilege in the judgment to the chosen race. The spiritual blindness of the privileged nation, or of its religious leaders, would have the effect of excluding them from the Kingdom. When Jesus wept over Jerusalem he foresaw the end of the special opportunity which the providence of God had assigned to the Jew. "O Jerusalem, Jerusalem, which killeth the prophets and stoneth them that are sent unto her! How often would I have gathered thy children together, even as a hen gathereth her chickens under her wings, and ye would not! Behold, your house is left unto you desolate." [1] The divine judgment upon the House of Israel has already begun. In the rejection of the present Kingdom, as manifested in himself, Jesus sees the impending rejection of the "sons of the Kingdom" from the glory of the consummation. Closely connected with the rejection of those who considered themselves to be by birth heirs of the Kingdom is the inclusion of those who were considered to be outcasts from it. In that great day, Jesus says, "Many shall come from the East and the West and shall sit down with Abraham, and Isaac and Jacob in the Kingdom of Heaven, but

[1] Matthew xxiii. 37, 38. Luke xiii. 34, 35.

the sons of the Kingdom shall be cast forth into the outer darkness." [1]

In the Parable of the Great Feast Jesus told a story of a man who prepared a banquet only to find that his invited guests, on various pretexts, refused to come. Thereupon he sent out messengers to bring in the uninvited and disreputable that his feast might be furnished with guests.[2] There are two versions of this parable and that according to Luke includes two separate expeditions by messengers to fill the places left vacant by those originally invited. Perhaps they stand for the missions to outcast Jews and to the Gentiles,[3] but, in any case, the purpose of the parable is plainly to emphasize the exclusion of the privileged and the inclusion of those who had no special religious advantages—of the outsiders in the eyes of the orthodox.

We are reminded once again of the identity of the Kingdom present and active here and now with the Kingdom which is to come in power hereafter. The final judgment is only a ratification and conclusion of that judgment which is being passed on men by their actions and decisions every day. If we ask, what is the quality of disposition and character which finally excludes from the Kingdom and incurs the condemnation to "outer darkness", we have two answers which, though at first sight different, turn out, on examination, to be in agreement. When Jesus was accused of being able to cast out demons by the power

[1] Matthew viii. 12.

[2] Matthew xxii. 1–13. Luke xiv. 16–24.

[3] Cf. Dodd, *Parables of the Kingdom*, p. 121.

of Beelzebub, after dwelling upon the absurdity of supposing that "Satan could cast out Satan", he went on to utter words which have been the subject of much anxious reflection among Christians. "Verily I say unto you all their sins shall be forgiven unto the sons of men, and their blasphemies wherewith soever they shall blaspheme, but whosoever shall blaspheme against the Holy Spirit hath never forgiveness, but is guilty of an eternal sin."[1] The evangelist adds as comment, "Because they said, He hath an unclean spirit." The essential nature of this "eternal sin" is clear enough. It consists in so utterly turning against the action of God in men and the working of the Holy Spirit as to attribute the divine inspiration to the forces of evil. It is a reversal of values so complete that the victim of this spiritual necrosis is unable to see anything but evil in the highest good. We hear in these words the echo of the prophet's cry, "Woe unto them that call evil good and good evil"; but the state of soul referred to is not that which may admit a theoretical doubt concerning the true values of life or express itself in verbal blasphemy; it is a settled and inveterate habit of mind, which is not only impervious to the appeal of goodness but by its inmost bias and fixed inclination reacts against it. Such a character has taken a final part against the Kingdom of God and has become, in the strict sense, diabolical. We are not to suppose that Jesus intended to assert that his opponents and accusers on this occasion had actually committed an eternal sin and were beyond the pale of God's mercy, but rather that he solemnly

[1] Mark iii. 28, 29 and parallels.

warned them of the danger of the course into which their prejudices had hurried them.

One of the sayings which is best attested of all that Jesus spoke is that to which we have already referred: "Whosoever shall be ashamed of me and of my words in this adulterous and sinful generation the Son of Man will be ashamed of him when he comes in the glory of the Father with the holy angels." [1] We have no less than five different versions of this word in the Synoptic Gospels and there is little doubt that it represents an idea which was constantly recurring in the teaching of Jesus. [2] The way in which a man responds to Jesus himself is the standard by which he will be judged. To be prepared for utter devotion to the Son of Man and his good news is the way to inherit the life of the age to come. "Whosoever would save his life shall lose it and whosoever shall lose his life for my sake and that of the good news shall save it. For what doth it profit a man to gain the whole world and forfeit his life?" [3] The position which a man takes up with regard to the Kingdom which has come with Jesus determines his place in the Kingdom which is to come, in the eternal Kingdom. This overwhelming claim which Christ makes and its consequences are not out of harmony with the teaching on the sin against the Holy Spirit. On the contrary, we have here another aspect of the same thought. The utter and final rejection of Jesus is the refusal to recognize the highest good, the divine life manifested

[1] Mark viii. 38.

[2] Cf. Matthew xvi. 27 f. Luke ix. 26 f. Matthew x. 32, 33. Luke xii. 8, 9.

[3] Mark viii. 35, 36.

in action. When carried to its conclusion it issues in a complete separation from the source of life. Of course this saying and others of a similar import presuppose that the individual has actually been presented with the alternative and that the great refusal has been made with a knowledge of the issue. Jesus is speaking of "this sinful and adulterous generation" in which his ministry was exercised. There, as he himself remarks, the effect of his work is to produce division, to set members of the same family at variance, to bring not peace but a sword. Men are already being distinguished into two groups by the necessity of decision.

It need scarcely be said that the teaching which we have been reviewing on the judgment of men and the issue of spiritual life and death has very little to do with the profession of orthodox beliefs. The Church has attached anathemas to its creeds and insisted that a right faith on such subjects as the Incarnation and the Trinity is necessary for those who would not perish everlastingly. Without questioning the value of correct theological doctrine, we may observe that "to confess" Jesus before men means primarily a personal adherence, the becoming one of the "little flock" which followed him and shared his life. From this discipleship doubtless sprang beliefs, and specially the belief that he was the Messiah. In the earliest days theology emerged from life as the formulation of an experience which was created in those who heard the command, "Follow me", and obeyed.

The Kingdom of God then will be, in its final and glorious advent, first of all the judgment of God upon the world, or rather the completion of that judgment which the present Kingdom among men is already bringing to pass. The final defeat of the powers of evil, which Jesus saw in the moment of triumph, " Satan fallen as lightning from heaven ", will be accomplished. Of the conditions of the triumphant Kingdom Jesus speaks little. Those who attain to it will be " as the angels ", and earthly conditions, such as marriage, will be transcended. The principles, however, of that Kingdom are clear enough. In it the sovereignty of God is complete and perfect. When His Kingdom comes, His will is done in earth as it is in heaven—throughout the whole of creation. The state of those who enter it may be described as " eternal life ". Eternal life is, in fact, a synonym of the Kingdom. " How hardly shall those that have riches enter the Kingdom " is Jesus' comment on the rich young ruler who had asked what he should do to inherit eternal life. That the Kingdom, not only in the present world but in the age to come, includes fellowship, may be gathered from the fact that Jesus adopts the very common Apocalyptic symbol of a feast. More than once in his parables he employs the image of a meal to illustrate the Kingdom and, as we shall see, it is present in his mind at the Last Supper.

In this chapter we have been moving among ideas which are strange to the modern world. There are some who would expunge all the concepts which have an apocalyptic flavour and ancestry from the teaching of Jesus, but this can be done only by a criticism so drastic and so arbitrary that we should have nothing on which we could securely base our estimate of the

Teacher. Others would hold that the images and " ideograms " of the Kingdom were indeed used by Jesus but that he imparted to them a new and more spiritual sense, which was, to a large extent, not understood by his disciples. This is undoubtedly true. We have already seen, and shall see more fully later, that the teaching of Jesus is profoundly and decisively different from that of the Apocalypses as it is from that of the Prophets. But it is difficult to see how we can avoid the conclusion that Jesus looked forward to a great consummation of the age and the coming of the Son of Man at the end of history. The witness of primitive Christianity is surely almost decisive on this point. Unless the earliest documents are utterly false, Christianity in its first years was full of the expectation of the Parousia, of the coming of Christ to judge. The earliest Christian writing known to us, the first of St. Paul's epistles to the Thessalonians, was written before the great Apostle had developed his own highly original and profound interpretation of the gospel and may be supposed to represent " what he had received ", the teaching common to all Christians. There we read: " For this we say unto you by the word of the Lord that we that are alive, that are left unto the coming of the Lord, shall in no wise precede them that are fallen asleep. For the Lord himself shall descend from heaven, with a shout, with the voice of the archangel and with the trump of God; and the dead in Christ shall rise first; then we that are alive, that are left, shall together with them be caught up in the clouds to meet the Lord in the air; and so shall we ever be with the Lord."[1]

[1] I Thessalonians iv. 15–17.

We seem almost compelled to conclude that the expectation of the primitive Church that Christ would speedily return " in the clouds of heaven " was based upon the teaching of Jesus himself, and though we are rightly reminded that the words of the Lord may have been misinterpreted in part and that there was a tendency in the first generation of Christians to heighten the apocalyptic imagery, there is every reason to believe that he spoke of the coming triumph of the Kingdom in terms which indicate that he expected the end to be shortly after his death.

It is not the purpose of this book to treat of Christian theology and we must therefore refrain from commenting on the problems which are raised for the modern believer. It is, however, relevant to point out that the problem is not new. The fact that the Parousia did not happen, at least in the form which men believed they had the warrant of the Lord's own words for anticipating, was in early times a great crisis for faith. " Where is the promise of his coming?" was anxiously asked by Christians of the first and second centuries. There have been many answers, but the most daring and profound is in the New Testament itself. The Gospel of John gives the eternal significance, as it seems to the author, of the Second Coming and the Judgment. They are not external events but spiritual realities. Christ comes again in the outpouring of the Spirit in the Church; the judgment is a continuous process and every day is the day of the Lord: " For God sent not the Son into the world to judge the world but that the world should be saved through him. He that believeth on him is not judged: he that believeth not hath been judged already, because he hath not believed on the name of the only-begotten Son of God. And this is the judgment that the light is come into the world and men loved darkness rather than the light, for their works were evil."[1]

[1] John iii. 17–19.

VI

THE LIFE OF THE SONS OF THE KINGDOM

THAT Jesus of Nazareth is among the world's greatest ethical teachers is a proposition which would gain almost universal assent, yet, in one sense of the words " ethical teacher ", it is untrue. He has no ethical system to promulgate. He does not show how the duties and virtues can be deduced from some general principle; nor is he interested in finding a logical definition of " the good " or of qualities of human character, such as courage, which are regarded as valuable. A comparison has often been made between Jesus and Socrates, suggested no doubt by the fact that both were victims of the orthodoxy of the time, but though the comparison may be illuminating in certain respects, it may also be most misleading, for there is a profound difference in spirit between the patron saint of rationalism and the Son of Man. The former seeks for an understanding of the nature of the good, in order that human life and conduct may be regulated by reason, the latter speaks magisterially about human life from the standpoint of one who stands in a unique relation with God. In their death they are most obviously both alike and dissimilar. Both died voluntarily in the sense that they could have escaped their fate; both died in the service of a cause which was worthy of their sacrifice; but Socrates died rather than violate the laws of the city, a martyr to civic virtue, while Jesus died for the sake of the Kingdom of God, giving his life as a " ransom on behalf of many ".

Since the time of Kant, who inaugurated at the close of the eighteenth century the modern period of thought, it has been a commonly accepted opinion among philosophers that ethics is " autonomous ". That is to say, it has been held that morality does not depend upon anything extraneous to itself, on the beliefs or disbeliefs, for example, which the individual may have about religion or politics. The judgments of the conscience, or of the " practical reason ", have no need, according to this view, of any further support; they are true and valid in their own right. This separation of ethics from religion, metaphysics and politics is a modern conception. The ancient world was very far from holding it. To the men of the old culture conduct was intimately connected with either religion or politics or with both. Plato does not consider it possible to discuss the nature of righteousness or of the truly righteous man without discussing the nature of the really just city and also, in the end, the nature of existence itself. Though Aristotle treated of ethics in a separate work, he makes it abundantly clear that the theory of right conduct for the individual cannot be divorced from the theory of politics—the meaning of the good " polis " or city. There are signs that this idea of the autonomy of ethics is waning in influence. Marxist Communism has reaffirmed the close connexion of conduct in the individual with political and economic movements. Perhaps the strange situation in which Christianity and Atheistic Communism find themselves has some relation with their attitude to morality. They are enemies, and necessarily so, yet they understand one another better than they understood the rationalism of the nineteenth century. Both find the basis of ethics beyond the ethical consciousness. For Marxism there are ultimately no values but economic values; for Christianity, in the end, all values are religious.

For Jesus there is no distinction between religion and morality. His moral teaching grows out of his belief in God—or rather from his experience of God. The point has often been made, but it is of great importance to emphasize it again because we have always with us amiable persons who imagine that they can take the moral teaching of Jesus and regard it as an independent doctrine, which has only an accidental connexion with the ideas which he happened to hold about God and the Kingdom of God. It can only be said that such an artificial precipitate from the Gospels utterly misrepresents the thought of Jesus. His teaching on conduct springs directly from his teaching about God.

In this respect, it need not be said, Jesus is in complete agreement with the Hebrew Prophets, and indeed with the whole of the Old Testament. To him, as to any Jew of his time, a separation even in thought between religion and morality was inconceivable. We are not here concerned with the general question of the truth of this belief nor with the philosophical problem of the relation between religion and ethics, but it may be remarked in passing that to common sense it would seem obvious that the question what kind of conduct is really good has a close connexion with the question what kind of world this really is, and that again is bound up with the questions is there a God and what is the nature of God?

The root idea of Hebrew ethics is that righteousness means obedience to and conformity with the will of God. The right action is right because it is the action which fulfils the law of God, the good man is good just in so far as he obeys the divine will. Thus good actions are not good because they are in some way rational, or convenient or expedient, though in fact they may be all these, but because they correspond to the will of God. At the time when Jesus taught, the will of God was found supremely in the Law of Moses, the Torah, which, by general agreement, was the ultimate sanction of all righteousness. The religion and ethics of the Jews at the beginning of the Christian era was probably the supreme instance of an attempt to regulate the whole of life by a code which had divine authority. The words " law " and " legal " have depressing and repressive associations; we tend to regard all law as a necessary evil. Nothing, however, would have been farther from the mind of the Jew than such an attitude. To him the possession of the " Law of the Lord his God " was the great privilege which marked him off as a member of the chosen race and distinguished him from every other nation. That the study and contemplation of the law could be a source of spiritual religion, in which joy and gratitude are present, is sufficiently shown by familiar verses in the Psalms. " What delight have I in thy law." " Thy law is more precious to me than gold and silver." " All the day long is my study in it." Such phrases as these doubtless represent the genuine feeling of many a scribe and of humbler people who found in the Law a food for the soul.

The Law of Moses, as we know it in the Old Testament, contains ritual and ceremonial regulations, moral directions, and a civil code. But minute as, in many respects, its injunctions are, they could not as they stood cover the whole of life. The conditions had changed since the Law assumed definitive form and many of its precepts were appropriate to a life which had passed. But, beyond this, there is a standing difficulty which attends every attempt to regulate the whole of life by a code. Life is too complex to be fitted into the frame of a legal system, and inevitably there occur cases which are either not covered by any law or where there seems to be a conflict of laws. Thus there arises a method of interpreting the code which is really an extension of it. The law is stretched by what is ostensibly an explanation or comment to cases which had really never been contemplated in the original enactments. This had happened on a large scale in the Jewish religion. Alongside the Law of Moses was a body of the " Traditions of the Elders ", as Jesus calls it, which had more or less the authority of the Laws of God.

The Pharisees represented that party in the community which pushed reverence for the Law of Moses to the extreme point. In the Gospels they appear almost invariably in an unfavourable light and their hostility to Jesus was, beyond question, a main cause of the crucifixion. But even in the Gospels there are indications that the Pharisees were not wholly bigoted and obstructive, and it is only just to remember that the ideal for which they stood was not an ignoble one. The New Testament was written by their enemies and we should allow for this fact when estimating their aims. The best Pharisees were inspired by the conception that all life, down to its most minute details, could be sacred, a thought which, in another form, has been of great influence in Christianity. Thus they held that the Law of God must regulate every action so that every part of conduct should be " filled with sacredness ". As we have seen, the ideal was impossible and the attempt to realize it led to a stiff legalism against which Jesus uttered a memorable protest; but in judging the Pharisees we may say, in the words of Jesus on the cross, that the best among them " knew not what they did ".

Closely associated with the conception of the Law of God was that of the Covenant between God and his people. The Covenant was never, in the Old Testament, described as a bargain in which each side obtains advantages. The special relation set up by the Covenant was a result of the unmerited love of Jehovah for the nation, an act of free choice, but it involved obligations on the part of the chosen people to keep the ordinances of God and to serve no other God. The Law is the standing witness of the Covenant, the keeping of the Law is the duty which is imposed as the condition of privilege.

In one fundamental respect Jesus does not depart from the standpoint of the Jewish religion. To be righteous means for him, as it meant to the Pharisees and all Jews, to do the will of God. There could be no more striking evidence of this than his own exclamation when in agony in the Garden of Gethsemane; facing the prospect of his own sacrificial death, after praying that if it were possible the cup should pass from him, he adds, " not my will but thine be done ". To obey the will of God, even when the purpose of that will is inscrutable, is the way of righteousness. The difference, and it is profound enough, is that Jesus does not find the complete and final revelation of the will of God in the Law and the traditions of the elders. He himself, by a direct intuition, knows the will of God and declares it. With an authority equal to that of Moses he states the meaning of righteousness. " Heaven and earth shall pass away, but my words shall not pass away." [1]

Thus Jesus is, in one sense, a new lawgiver. The Gospel of Matthew evidently intends its readers to understand this from the setting of the Sermon on the Mount. As Moses received the old Law on Sinai, so Jesus proclaims the new Law from the mount. " It was said to them of old time . . . but I say unto you." St. Paul, though he held that the gospel had superseded the Law, can still speak of the moral teaching of Jesus as a law. " Bear ye one another's burdens and so fulfil the law of Christ." [2] The moral teaching of Jesus is intended for those who have entered the Kingdom, for the people of God, for the

[1] Mark xiii. 31. [2] Galatians vi. 2.

faithful " remnant ", for the new Israel. They are distinguished from those who are outside the Kingdom by the fact that they fulfil the new law of the new Israel. " Ye know that they which are accounted to rule over the Gentiles lord it over them and their great ones exercise authority over them, but it is not so among you; but whosoever would wish to become great among you shall be your servant and whosoever would wish to be first among you shall be your slave."[1] " A new commandment I give unto you, that ye love one another; as I loved you that ye also love one another. By this shall all men know that ye are my disciples, if ye have love one to another."[2]

The righteousness of those who are entering the Kingdom is not so much a new kind of righteousness as one which goes beyond that required and approved by the accredited exponents of the Law. " Except your righteousness shall exceed that of the scribes and Pharisees ye shall in no wise enter into the Kingdom of Heaven."[3] The law of the Kingdom is, so to speak, the ancient holiness of Israel carried to its logical conclusion. This means that the goodness which Jesus regards as the only one truly deserving the name is that of " the heart ", of the disposition and motives. That this is both a fulfilment of the Law and also a revolutionary change is evident enough. The law is not really obeyed so long as the inner consent of the mind is lacking, and the true judgment of the moral value of a man must be based upon the direction of his desires and will. This was not unknown to the higher religious minds of Judaism and

[1] Mark x. 42, 43. [2] John xiii. 34, 35. [3] Matthew v. 20.

is indeed a common theme of the Prophets. "This people honoureth me with their lips but their heart is far from me." But the application of this truth to the system of legal righteousness is, in the end, destructive of the whole conception of righteousness through the law. The attempt to conform to an elaborate code necessarily concentrates attention on the outward acts, for they alone can be the subjects of exact legislation. A righteousness which is of the inner spirit demands a change of mind, a repentance which transforms the man himself. "The good man out of the good treasure of his heart bringeth forth that which is good and the evil man out of the evil treasure bringeth forth that which is evil; for out of the abundance of the heart his mouth speaketh."[1] "From within, out of the heart of men, evil thoughts proceed, fornications, thefts, murders, adulteries, covetings, wickedness, deceit, lasciviousness, an evil eye, railing, pride, foolishness: all these evil things proceed from within and defile the man."[2]

The change of mind which is necessary for those who would enter the Kingdom consists of a complete revolution in values. In contrast to "those who are without" the Son of the Kingdom must estimate as good much which the almost universal consent of mankind agrees to regard as evil, and much as evil which is commonly accepted as good. Jesus enforces this in a series of moral paradoxes so startling that they have been the constant embarrassment of the Church in its necessary compromise with civilization. The poor are blessed and it is dangerous to have wealth.

[1] Luke vi. 45. Matthew xii. 35. [2] Mark vii. 21–23.

If we adopt Matthew's version of this beatitude and read "poor in spirit" the meaning is not essentially different. Those who have no desire to assert themselves or demand their just rights are fitted for the Kingdom. The meek and the persecuted are the truly happy, because their disposition is that which the Kingdom requires. Resistance to the evil man is not permitted to the disciple. "Ye have heard that it was said, An eye for an eye and a tooth for a tooth; but I say unto you Resist not him that is evil but whosoever smiteth thee on thy right cheek, turn to him the other also. And if any man would go to law with thee and take away thy coat, let him have thy cloke also. And whosoever shall compel thee to go one mile, go with him twain. Give to him that asketh thee and from him that would borrow turn thou not away. . . . I say unto you, Love your enemies and pray for them that persecute you, that ye may be sons of your Father who is in heaven."[1] The disciple is to refrain from judgment of others if he himself would escape judgment.

These words are so familiar that we easily overlook their real significance. Not only are they hard to carry out—they are impossible, if we take them in their literal significance. They strike at the root of every society. It is quite inadequate to say that they are a condemnation of the brutal social order which was in existence at the time of Jesus: they condemn any society which has existed or could exist. Thus, for example, it is often rightly pointed out that the moral teaching of Jesus utterly prohibits war, but the fact

[1] Matthew v. 38–45. Luke vi. 29, 30.

is that it goes very much farther. The evil man is not to be resisted at all. The use of force, whether through police or other means, to restrain the anti-social individual is even more clearly prohibited than war by the words of Jesus. The tyrant is indeed utterly outside the pale of the Kingdom as Jesus conceives it; but no less certainly is the revolutionary who overthrows the tyrant. Again, any social order, even the most communistic, must have some law of property and guarantee some right to the individual, but if we keep to the plain meaning of Christ's words, it is evident that the man who enters the Kingdom will take no measures to protect his rights or his property nor will he assist in the preservation of order by judging his fellow man. We must surely agree with Professor Whitehead when he says that the adoption of the principles of the Sermon on the Mount, literally understood, on any large scale would mean the "sudden death" of civilization.

What is the significance of this? It is clear that the kind of life which Jesus depicts in the Sermon on the Mount is one which has transcended the life in any earthly society. The perfect son of the Kingdom has left behind the whole circle of ideas which are inherent in any imperfect social group. He is no longer a member of a community of persons having claims one upon another which can be enforced; he has gone beyond justice. He makes no claim for himself; he does not assert either himself or his rights. In the eyes of the world he is poor in spirit. We must always remember that these were no merely theoretical maxims in the mouth of Jesus. He acted upon them.

He had nowhere to lay his head, " when he was reviled he reviled not again, when he suffered, threatened not." [1]

The difficulty which arises in applying the precepts of the Sermon on the Mount to the life of the citizen has been met in more than one way. An ancient theory in the Church is that of the " two standards " which are distinguished as " commands of the Lord " and " counsels of perfection ". According to this view, there are two levels of spiritual and moral attainment. The life lived in the world may be thoroughly Christian in that it is inspired by love of God and of one's neighbour while accepting the normal conditions of society including the legal and commercial system. There is, however, a more heroic mode of love which gives itself to the Lord without any reserve, renouncing all property, all just claims for the self and every comfort which society can give. On this basis has been founded the monastic ideal and the belief that the life of the " religious " may be more perfect than that of the Christian in the world. Protestant writers have denounced this theory of the two standards as plainly contrary to the teaching of Jesus, but there is really much more to be said for it than they allow. Several sayings of Jesus indicate that he recognized as good and even as deserving of " reward " persons who certainly fell short of the demands of the Sermon on the Mount. There were some who were " not far from the Kingdom of God ". He can say that " he that is not against us is for us. For whosoever shall give you a cup of cold water to drink because ye are Christ's, verily I say unto you he shall in no wise

[1] 1 Peter ii. 23.

lose his reward ".[1] The picture of the Judgment which is sometimes called the Parable of the Sheep and Goats is found only in Matthew and must therefore be referred to with caution. If it is a genuine saying of Jesus, it reiterates the thought that service to even the least of the brethren of Jesus will qualify for entrance at the last to the Kingdom " prepared from the foundation of the world ".[2]

In recent years another explanation of the ethical teaching of Jesus has been put forward by those who stress the apocalyptic element in his outlook to the exclusion of others equally important. It is argued that the ethic of Jesus is an " ethic for the interim "; in other words, that the whole of his thought on conduct is dominated by the belief that the end of the age is imminent. The theory has at least a plausible appearance. It is able to explain the apparent indifference of Jesus to the social and political situation and to represent the most paradoxical sayings as really not paradoxical at all. There is no need to resist the evil man; before long he will be abolished by the final Judgment. There is no time to care for clothes or property: they will be useless in the Kingdom of the Messiah. The implications of this theory would obviously be far-reaching, for it might well be urged that a doctrine which was reasonable enough in a world about to be destroyed could have no meaning for those who are living in a world which they expect to continue. A mere " ethic of the interim " would be useless for us who do not expect history to end to-morrow.

The idea that Jesus' ethics are wholly determined

[1] Mark ix. 41. [2] Matthew xxv. 31–46.

by the belief in an imminent end of the age is not supported by the evidence. Not one of the most startling sayings of the Lord about conduct is supported by any reference to the shortness of the time. It would have been natural to add such a reason, and in fact this very reason is given for the necessity of watching and praying. Nor can it be said that the oracular manner of Jesus' utterance precluded the appeal to supporting considerations, for in various cases he does give them—and they are not the considerations which the theory of "interim ethics" would expect. Thus the warning against anxiety is based on the fatherly care of God. Again, in his teaching on marriage and divorce Jesus makes no reference to the shortness of the time as St. Paul does in a similar context. He bases his doctrine on the original divine purpose, "From the beginning of the creation male and female made he them."[1] When he forbids his disciples to be called "Rabbi" he does not urge that such titles and salutations are senseless in view of the rapid approach of the catastrophe; he adds "for one is your teacher and all ye are brethren".[2]

Professor Whitehead[3] has made an illuminating comment on the Sermon on the Mount in which he puts his finger on the element of truth in the "ethic for the interim" theory. He remarks that the apocalyptic setting of Jesus' thought enabled him to disregard consequences, to abstract his mind from the probable results of acting on the principles which he laid down, and thus to have "absolute ethical intuitions". Whereas we are constantly distracted

[1] Mark x. 6. [2] Matthew xxiii. 8.

[3] Cf. A. N. Whitehead, *Adventures of Ideas*, pp. 18 ff.

from the perception of what would be unconditionally right and good by the thought of what would happen to-morrow or next year, Jesus was able to see the good and right without any admixture and dilution of the expedient. This precise way of putting the point is open to criticism, and if Whitehead implies that Jesus' ethic was wholly conditioned by apocalyptic expectations we must demur, but the central thought is true and illuminating. In the utterances which sound to us so remote from the circumstances and necessities of our lives Jesus was describing the life which would be good, the only life which could be called good without qualification. The Beatitudes and the associated teaching awaken in our minds a longing for a life which is possible here and now only in faint shadow and approximation. And, still following Prof. Whitehead, we may add that thus is explained a strange characteristic of Christianity. Why has the religion which began with a teaching so little touched by the idea of progress been in fact the inspiration of the most progressive and restless civilization? It is because in the "absolute ethical intuitions of Jesus" it has had a standard by which progress must be measured and a constant vision of a life that might be. The only society which could satisfy would be one in which the Sermon on the Mount would be the norm of human living. The tension set up between the ideal and the actual has been the source both of Christian discontent and of Christian vitality. Always the deeper spirit of the Church has been crying, in the words which end Bernard Shaw's *St. Joan*, "How long, O Lord, before thy world is fit for thy saints!"

VII

JESUS AND THE LAW OF MOSES

WHAT attitude did Jesus take towards the Jewish Law? That there was a decisive difference between him and the Pharisees on this question is clear enough and there is ample evidence that he repudiated the " tradition of the elders " on the ground that it sometimes, in effect, annulled the true purpose of the Law and laid on simple folk burdens too heavy for them to bear. But it is not so clear that he definitely rejected the whole Law or encouraged his disciples to disregard it. There was doubt on this question in the early Church and the first great controversy in Christianity broke out on the subject of St. Paul's doctrine that the Law was now superseded by the gospel. It is clear that the primitive Christians were accustomed to obey the ceremonial law and, for some time, appeared to be a sect of people among the Jews who differed from their fellows chiefly by reason of their belief that the Messiah had already appeared in the person of Jesus and that he would come again. The elaborate argument by which St. Paul supports his conception of the Law and its function shows that the Church possessed no clear word of the Lord on the subject. The main contention of St. Paul is that the old way of righteousness by the Law has now been abolished by the new way of righteousness by faith in Christ. The Law was not in itself evil; on the contrary it was "holy and the commandment righteous and good".[1] But it did not procure salvation. It set a standard which could not be kept. In the providence of God, the Law had the purpose of arousing a consciousness of sin. It was a "tutor to bring us to Christ that we might be justified by faith".[2] We are not concerned here with the details of St. Paul's theology of the Law but with the belief, or rather experience, that there is a righteousness which consists not in conformity with a code but in the inward adhesion of the mind to Christ and the inspiration by the Holy Spirit. "As many as are led by the Spirit of God these are the sons of God."[3]

In our Gospels there are several expressions of respect both for the Law and for its accredited exponents. According to Matthew Jesus prefaced his denunciations of the Scribes and Pharisees by a sentence indicating respect for their authority. "The scribes and Pharisees sit on Moses seat; all things therefore that they bid you these do and observe; but do not ye after their works for they say and do not."[4] It is unlikely that this is a correct account of what Jesus said, because it is impossible to reconcile it with other words of certain authenticity. Jesus' quarrel with the teachers of the law went deeper than the accusation that they did not conform to their own doctrines. Matthew here no doubt reflects the opinion of those Christians who, unlike St. Paul, held to the Jewish

[1] Galatians iii. 19. [2] Galatians iii. 24.
[3] Romans viii. 14. [4] Matthew xxiii. 2, 3.

legal system. But there is better evidence that Jesus did not at least urge a sudden revolt against the practices of the ceremonial law. In St. Luke, whose Gospel represents the standpoint of Gentile Christianity and is the least Jewish in tone of the Synoptic writers, we read, "Woe unto you Pharisees! for ye tithe mint and rue and every herb and pass over judgment and the love of God; but these ought ye to have done and not to leave the other undone."[1] That Jesus kept the festivals of the Law is again evidence that he preached no open and decisive breach with the system. Just before his death he prepared to eat the Passover with his disciples. Only the Gospel of John depicts Jesus as in radical antagonism with "the Jews" from the first, and in this matter we must suppose that it carries back into the life of Jesus a situation which arose later in the development of the Church.

At least it is evident that, if Jesus did not advocate the abrogation of the ceremonial law, he treated it as of little importance. The principle on which it is to be judged is that of expediency. "The sabbath was made for man and not man for the Sabbath." "Is it lawful to do good on the Sabbath or to do harm, to save a life or to destroy it?"[2] Ritual and ceremonial requirements must give way before the weightier matters, righteousness and mercy: they have value only so far as they further the true life of man.

The decisive passage for the question of Jesus' view of the ritual law is that which recounts the controversy with Pharisees and certain scribes, who had come from Jerusalem, on the question of ceremonial purity.

[1] Luke xi. 42. [2] Luke vi. 9. Mark iii. 4.

"Why walk not thy disciples according to the tradition of the elders but eat their bread with defiled hands?" The question indicates that, in the circle of disciples, the minutiæ of the law were disregarded. After showing that tradition had sometimes the effect of "making void the word of God", Jesus called the crowd and said: "Hear me all of you and understand; there is nothing from without the man, that going into him can defile him; but the things which proceed out of the man are those that defile the man." [1] The introductory words indicate that Jesus regarded this as a matter of supreme importance which it was necessary for all to understand. As Dr. Rashdall remarks, they "cut away at a stroke the whole principle of Jewish legalism". The evangelist comments on the utterance, "This he said making all meats clean". The "table laws" of Judaism were, in the ordinary affairs of life, its most distinctive feature. The restrictions upon food and the manner of eating were the characteristics which marked off the Jew in practice from all other men. The Temple at Jerusalem and its sacrifices were the centre of the Jewish religion, but they played little part in the lives of the majority of Jews, who were remote from the Holy City. In the disputes over the Law which troubled the churches founded by St. Paul, the controversy came to a head on this very point. St. Paul felt compelled to rebuke St. Peter because he withdrew from "table fellowship" with the non-Jewish brethren. "In uttering these memorable words our Lord was practically cancelling the whole system of the Mosaic Law and

[1] Mark vii. 14–23.

its ancient taboos and he could not have been altogether unconscious of this tendency. . . . In the words of Loisy, 'The emancipation of Paul, much more apparent, was not more real.'"[1]

To sum up this question: Jesus was no revolutionary either in political or ecclesiastical affairs. He believed that the Law and the Prophets were a revelation of God and he had no desire to lead a revolt against the system which was established. On the other hand, he read the Law and the Prophets with a spiritual insight unknown even to the best rabbis. The Law and the Prophets to him were not all equally valuable. Beneath their letter he discerned their spirit and distinguished between the permanent religious truths which they contained and the superficial and temporary elements which accompanied them. In short, Jesus read the Old Testament with the mind of a prophet and not with that of an exegete. Though he had no programme of religious revolt, his attitude towards the Law was, in fact, revolutionary. The distinction between the unimportant ceremonial laws and the inner spirit and intention of the Old Testament as a whole, if it had been accepted by the leaders of Judaism, might have transformed that religion, not by a sudden break, but by a new creative movement from within. This did not happen, and the historical consequence of the seed planted by Jesus was the Christian Church of the Gentiles, standing over against the Jewish people which held strictly and blindly to the Law.

[1] Rashdall, *The Idea of Atonement*, pp. 16, 17.

VIII

LOVE FULFILS THE LAW

WHEN Jesus was asked which is the first commandment of all he replied by quoting the " Shema ", the verse in Deuteronomy which forms the fundamental creed of the Jewish religion to this day. " Hear, O Israel, the Lord our God, the Lord is one, and thou shalt love the Lord thy God with all thy heart and with all thy soul, and with all thy mind and with all thy strength."[1] He went on to add a second, which he quoted again from the Law: " The second is this, Thou shalt love thy neighbour as thyself."[2] This answer was greatly approved by the scribe who had put the question and Mark tells us that Jesus said to him, " Thou art not far from the Kingdom of God ". Luke gives a different version of the incident, in which the saying is attributed to the questioner and approved by Jesus, and forms an introduction to the parable of the Good Samaritan, which is told in answer to the inquiry, " Who is my neighbour?" These facts, familiar enough to readers of the New Testament, have several instructive implications. We find here Jesus in amicable conversation with a scribe and in agreement with him on the essential

[1] Mark xii. 28–34. Matthew xxii. 37. Deuteronomy vi. 4, 5.
[2] Leviticus xix. 18.

commandments of the law, which supports the suggestion, made in the last chapter, that Jesus hoped to transform Judaism from within. The summary of the Law is itself quoted from the Law; to the monotheistic creed of all Jews is joined the passage from Leviticus. Whether this had ever been done before is perhaps not certain, but it is worthy of note that the learned Jewish commentator, Dr. Montefiore, quotes no parallel. Here we have the supreme example of the reverence of Jesus for the Law and also of his manner of interpreting it, not by anxious discussion of the letter but by the spirit of prophetic discernment. The passage in Leviticus meant by "neighbour" a member of the Hebrew nation and possibly also "the stranger within the gates", but it is possible that a wider interpretation was given to the word by the more liberal Jews in the time of Jesus, and it may have been the motive of the question, Who is my neighbour? to enlist the support of Jesus to one side or other of a controversy. The parable of the Prodigal Son does not answer the question; no theoretical decision can be deduced from it on the legal question, To whom do my duties to the neighbour extend? Instead we have a story of compassion shown by one who was regarded as outside the family of Israel. The point of the story is that he did not stop to ask, Who is my neighbour? So the love of which Jesus speaks goes out to those who are in need and stays not to ask whether they fall under the correct definition of neighbour.

It is noteworthy that Jesus finds the spirit of the Law in two precepts which are not in their nature legal. They cannot be treated as if they referred to acts which could be done or left undone. Though they give rise to actions, they are themselves dispositions of the mind and directions of the will. And if they are regarded as obligations, they are of unlimited extent. No one can say, " I have fulfilled them; I have loved God with my whole heart and my neighbour as myself ". They lay upon the man who accepts them a duty which is never finished, or, as we should rather say, they furnish him with an inspiration which is never exhausted. St. Paul had this in mind when he wrote, " Owe no man anything but to love one another ", for loving the neighbour is a debt which can never be completely paid off. Thus in his summing up of the Law Jesus transcends law, or perhaps it would be more accurate to say he shows how the Law contained in itself the principle of its own transcendence. He takes moral endeavour beyond the sphere of legalism and firmly establishes it as the activity of a free spirit guided by two closely linked principles. We must remind ourselves once again that, in doing so, Jesus was carrying further and giving precise form to a thought which was not strange to the nobler spirits of the Hebrew race, that thought which found its most memorable utterance in Jeremiah's prophecy of the New Covenant under which God would write his laws in the hearts of men.

The love for God is bound up with the love of God for men. It is the response which the child makes to the affection and care of the Father. As Dr. Manson has excellently insisted, the deep experience of Jesus, not only of the reality of God but of his own filial relation with the Father, is the source from which the teaching springs. To Jesus the love of the Father was a fact of immediate apprehension, so that it is for him an unquestioned postulate, and the response to the Father's love by the son is the natural consequence. From this insight all the teaching of Jesus flows.

The two great commandments are joined together and may not be put asunder. The fatherhood of God is the ground of the brotherhood of men—not simply the logical ground but the spring from which it rises in the heart as a motive for conduct. The child turning in love to the Father cannot forget the other children of the same Father and must include them in his circle of interest. But further, we cannot truly or safely love the neighbour unless we first love God. To love one's neighbour as oneself may be a dangerous maxim if one loves oneself wrongly, and some of the tragedies of love are due to the fact that the lover has indeed loved the object of his affection in the same manner as he loves himself. Only in so far as we love God first can we love our neighbour with a love which is creative and not destructive. In Balzac's novel *Père Goriot* is presented a heart-rending story of the love of a father for his daughters. Certainly Goriot loved them at least as much as he loved himself, but in this modern Lear, as the great novelist draws him, there was no hint of any love of God or of reverence for values which are larger than personal gratification. The love of Goriot, in the end, destroyed not only himself but the higher natures of the daughters as well. One of the deepest injuries which sentimentalists have done to Christianity is to suggest that Jesus was foolish enough to believe that a vague exhortation to love one another would produce any effect and that, if the natural man, without any change of mind through love of God, could be induced to love his neighbours, any great good would come of it. At least in the teaching of Jesus to love God is the first and great commandment.

We see then that any attempt to classify Jesus as a "humanist" can only be due to a profound misunderstanding of his central conviction. And this remark applies also to most of the philosophical systems of ethics which have claimed to give a more abstract or "rational" version of his doctrine of love of the neighbour. The essence of Christianity has been supposed to be the "principle of benevolence", a worthy though somewhat cold favourite of the eighteenth century. Some have believed that the core of Christian ethics was formulated by Kant in the rational maxim, "Treat personality, whether in thyself or others, always as an end and never as a means only". J. S. Mill contended that in the catchword of Utilitarianism, "everyone to count for one and no one for more than one", the really valuable element in Christianity had been epitomized. No doubt each of these formulas expresses an aspect or a consequence of Christ's teaching, but they are all very far from the truth if they are taken as adequate descriptions of the love of the neighbour as he understood it. For him it is not a rational principle but an attitude and direction of the mind and will, which arises from the relation of the soul with God. "We love because he first loved us." The love of the brethren is not just a good idea, or a reasonable way of acting, or an expedient mode of conduct, or a character to be cultivated for the general good. It is a gift of grace.

Three thoughts, therefore, lie at the root of all Jesus' teaching on ethics: the love of God for men; the response of the man to the love of God; the consequent love of the neighbour. Clearly it is important to gain some definite idea of the meaning of " love " in this context. Some light has already been thrown on this matter by the previous chapters, but the word " love " in English and in other languages is so ambiguous and has been used in so vague a manner in expositions of the teaching of Jesus that we may hope to learn something by a consideration of the meaning of the word used in the Gospels.

The word translated " love " in the New Testament is " agapē ", which is not the common Greek word. That word, " erōs ", does not occur in the New Testament. Moreover the word " agapē " is of so rare occurrence in Greek outside the Bible and Christian literature that it may be said to be a term brought into the vocabulary by the Biblical writers. These are the facts. What they mean is a matter of opinion. It has been said that " agapē " is a word created by Christianity, but this is not strictly accurate, for it is used in the Septuagint, the Greek translation of the Old Testament which was known to all the New Testament writers. It is, however, a significant thing that the New Testament deliberately discards the ordinary word and employs another. We may go further and conjecture with great probability that the reason for this was that " erōs " was felt to have associations which were not compatible with the Christian conception. Nor is it difficult to imagine what those associations were. " Erōs " is used, like the English word " love ", for an almost unlimited range of emotions and states of mind, but the root idea is that of desire and a sense of need. It has an intimate connexion with the instinct of sex. In its loftier signification the idea of sexual desire has been left behind and " erōs " acquires a philosophical and religious meaning. Thus Plato traces the ascent of the soul from the love of the beauty of earthly forms through the more intellectual kinds of loveliness to the Eternal Beauty—the supreme Good. Aristotle again conceives the universe as centred upon God, towards whom all things move as towards " an object of love or desire ". Love, in this sense, has been a motive force in much mystical religion which seeks, in its own normal phrase, for " union " with the divine. Psychologically speaking we might say that the development of the mystical consciousness is, on one side, a progressive sublimation of desire.

Professor Anders Nygren, in his important book, *Agape and Eros*, has recently offered some suggestive theories on the difference between the two conceptions indicated by the two words. He finds in their contrasted meanings the basis of two quite different types of religion. " Agapē ", in his view, has no associations with desire or sense of need. While we may call " erōs " in its higher meaning " man's way to God ", which starts from a sense of incompleteness and need, " agapē " is " God's way to man ", depending on no sense of need or lack but simply manifesting the undeserved good-will of the Father. Nygren goes so far as to speak of agapē as "unmotived" and "uncaused". The two kinds of religion which arise from the two kinds of love are, on the one hand, the mystical, which is essentially the ascent of the soul to God by the ladder of the purification of desire, and, on the other, the religion of grace, which rests upon the undeserved and "irrational" good-will of God, who gives, by his love, worth to that which in itself is of no value.

No doubt, this distinction between two types of religious experience is illuminating, but it seems too systematic and clear-cut to cover the facts. Mystical religion has not been devoid of all reliance upon the grace of God nor has it invariably conceived the spiritual pilgrimage as the steep ascent to God made by the unaided human spirit. On the contrary, it has believed that the beginning of the pilgrimage, the conversion, and all its stages were due to the life of God working in the human spirit. Nor has the religion of grace been destitute of the thought that in God alone the full life, the most desirable life, is to be found.

One point at least which arises from Prof. Nygren's discussion must be stressed. The love of which the Gospels speak is "irrational" in the sense that it does not depend on the actually existing value of the person loved. This is obviously true of the love of God for men. The generosity of the divine love is a salient element in Jesus' teaching. "He makes his rain fall on the just and on the unjust." Nothing again could be further from the kind of love which Jesus wishes to prevail among brethren than that nicely calculated affection which regulates itself according to the deserts of the object. A man who loved his mother less because she took to drink would be a most imperfect Christian. When Jesus entered into relations of friendship with Publicans and harlots it was not on account of their excellences of heart or head, and when he had compassion on the multitude it was not because the multitude was different from all other crowds; it was stupid, selfish and ignorant. Love is something which is given beyond what the object of love can claim as just. No one can say to another, and far less to God, I have a right to be loved because of what I am. "On ne prouve pas qu'on doit être aimé."[1] But in a deeper sense the love of which Jesus speaks is not "irrational". It depends upon an insight into the potentialities of persons. The self, as it actually is here and now, is not the whole self. There are hidden within it possibilities of development which have never yet been realized. Jesus looked on men as potential children of God and members of his Kingdom; he saw them in the light of God's purpose for them. And this is the love which is meant when we are told to love our neighbours as ourselves. To love ourselves as we are is the most deadly of sins; to love ourselves as God means us to be is the way of progress. So the merely natural affection, which often fastens on temporary and accidental traits in the beloved and would not have them change, may be a hindrance to the true growth of the loved one, while

[1] Pascal, *Pensées, II.*

the real agapē, which sees the beloved in the light of God's purpose, may be a means of grace and a sacrament of the love of God.

Is it true that " love " in the teaching of Jesus has no element of desire or sense of need? This obviously cannot be maintained when we are thinking of man's love for God. Jesus pronounces a beatitude on those who " hunger and thirst after righteousness ", which is really a blessing on those who, like the Psalmist, hunger and thirst after God. " As the hart panteth after the water brooks, so panteth my soul after thee, O God. My soul thirsteth for God, for the living God: when shall I come and appear before God?"[1] Jesus does not indeed speak of union with God as the goal of the soul's quest, but he refers in another beatitude to those who long to " appear before God ": " blessed are the pure in heart for they shall see God ". What again does the saying " Where your treasure is there will your heart be also "[2] imply except that the end towards which the disciple moves is a fulfilment, a satisfaction of need " in heaven " or with God?

If then the word " love " as used of man's love to God includes the idea of the fulfilment of the personality and the element of desire, we should expect that the same word would have similar associations when used of God's love for man. Though Christian theology has frowned on the idea that such conceptions as need and desire can rightly be used of God, it is the conviction of the present writer that the teaching of Jesus does plainly indicate that God needs man and yearns for man's response to love. The

[1] Psalm xlii. 1, 2. [2] Matthew vi. 21.

passages which support this view are among the most familiar in the Gospels and the common feeling that in them we have the very heart of Christ's message cannot be mistaken. The fatherhood of God is certainly not represented by Jesus as a passive quality. The love of the Father seeks out the lost. And in the parables which illuminate this seeking love, the Lost Sheep, the Lost Coin, and the Lost Son, there is included the joy of the finder. " There is joy in heaven likewise," we are told, " over one sinner that repents." The father's joy over the returned prodigal can scarcely be dismissed as an insignificant part of the story: it is in fact the point of the narrative. " It was meet to make merry and be glad, for this thy brother was dead and is alive again and was lost and is found." The opinion that need and the satisfaction of desire must not be attributed to God has respectable grounds which cannot be reviewed here, but they are philosophical in character and not based on the teaching of Christ. Jesus took the love of God seriously, and to him the divine fatherhood was more than inadequate metaphor. God is our Father, so he believed, even in the sense that he knows the most poignant of a father's experiences—the longing for an alienated and unloving child.

Love as the universal principle of conduct must evidently be something more than an emotional state. Real difficulties arise over the ethical teaching of Jesus when it is supposed that the second great commandment enjoins that we should have affectionate feelings towards all other human beings. The basis of the virtue, if such it can be called, is a settled will for the good of all our neighbours, which itself rests upon our faith in God's settled will for our good and theirs. But this will cannot effectively act, or even effectively exist, apart from the exercise of the imagination, which in P. E. More's phrase " grasps and makes real to ourselves the being of others ". The imagination is the link between will and emotion. A love of the neighbour which is on the way to perfection will glow with affectionate feeling even towards those who are by nature repulsive to us. This perfection of love is the quality of great saints, who have generally been also poets. Will, imagination and emotion have conspired together in them to create heroic love. That Jesus was felt to have this character is surely plain from the narratives in the Gospels. His works of healing were not simply acts of power to show forth his glory, as the Gospel of John seems to suggest; they were works of mercy called forth by the pitiful condition and the trust of the sufferers. In the account of the healing of the palsied man at Capernaum we have an indication of that insight into the mental condition of others which is the condition and also the consequence of love. He spoke first to the hidden trouble of the soul when he said, " Son, thy sins are forgiven ". The relation of the disciples to Jesus, so far as their motives are concerned, is a subject on which the Synoptic Gospels do not give us much information, but we may gather that the little band was often puzzled and nearly always lacking in comprehension of their Master but bound to him by the influence of a love which could not fail to win response. When Peter, after his denial of Jesus at the crisis of his fate, " went out and wept bitterly ", it was not because his faith in Jesus as Messiah had returned but because he had betrayed a friend who would never have betrayed him. John has accurately stated the situation when he reports Jesus as saying: " Even as my Father hath loved me, I also have loved you: abide ye in my love. . . . This is my commandment that ye love one another, even as I have loved you. Greater love hath no man than this that a man lay down his life for his friends."[1]

The assertion is sometimes heard that the ethic of Jesus is one of absolute self-sacrifice. Before we adopt this definition it is necessary to enquire what it means. An ethic which took self-sacrifice as the supreme good would presumably be one which aimed at the complete annihilation of the self and would regard the very existence of the self as an evil. There have been such theories. In some forms of Eastern mysticism the being of the individual is attributed to illusion and the spiritual progress of the saint consists in freeing himself by contemplation and ascetic practices from the illusion and so becoming one with the Divine or the Absolute. A somewhat similar theory is found in the philosophy of Buddhism. Nothing of this kind is to be discovered in the teaching of Jesus. In the absolute sense, his doctrine is not " life-negating " but " life-affirming ". As we read in John, " he is come that we might have life and have it more abundantly ". But the place of self-sacrifice in the life of the followers of Jesus is evidently so important that no one can be called a disciple unless he is pre-

[1] John xv. 9, 12, 13.

pared for the utmost surrender. "If any man would come after me let him deny himself and take up his cross daily and follow me." But these words are followed by others which show that the sacrifice is not an end in itself but a necessary means to a higher good—it is not for the sake of death but for the sake of life. "For whoseoever would save his life shall lost it, but whosoever shall lose his life for my sake shall save it. For what is a man profited if he gain the whole world and lose or forfeit his own self?"[1] Again the Second Commandment, on loving one's neighbour as oneself, presupposes that a certain love of the self is not only natural but right, for it would be senseless to recommend me to love my neighbour as myself and at the same time to say that I ought not to love myself at all. Further, we cannot ignore those sayings of Christ which refer to reward. We are to lay up treasure in heaven and the Father, who sees in secret, will reward us openly.

The solution of this apparent contradiction is to be found in the truth, plainly stated both by St. Paul and St. John, that the law of spiritual progress is life through death; we must die in order to live. "For ye died," says St. Paul, speaking of the conversion of the Colossians, "and your life is hid in Christ with God."[2] The only way by which the true self, the self which God purposes, can live is through the putting to death of the lower self with its narrowly personal interests and its constant claims for an exclusive satisfaction. Not until the limited self has been negated can a man's own self be realized. This

[1] Luke ix. 23–25. [2] Colossians iii. 3.

negation of the lower in order that the higher and more inclusive self may live, which is called by St. Paul "dying unto self and living unto Christ", is not an achievement of a moment, nor can it be wholly completed by a sudden conversion. The moment of choice is no doubt decisive when it can be known, but the process of dying in order to live is continuous. "I die daily," says St. Paul: "let a man deny himself and take up his cross daily and follow me," is the word of Jesus.

IX

THE FORGIVENESS OF SINS

THE movement of John the Baptist and his followers was concerned with the need for the forgiveness of sins, and the baptism which, in common with other Jewish sects, they practised was associated with the remission of guilt, though precisely how the ceremony was related with the spiritual benefit desired it is difficult to say. Those who came to John's baptism were anxious to escape the "wrath to come". This note of the need for forgiveness and the requirement of repentance sounds throughout the teaching of Jesus. In the prayer which he taught his disciples the petition for forgiveness of sins follows immediately on that for daily bread, the first need of the soul on the first need of the body. The subject of many parables is the readiness of God to forgive. We are led to believe that Jesus himself claimed the power to forgive sins and that this was a cause of scandal to the Pharisees. When he said, "Son, thy sins are forgiven", they commented, "Who can forgive sins but God alone?" Plainly we have here an indication of a difference between the activity of John and that of Jesus in the dealing with sin; Jesus, conscious that he was the Messiah, claimed himself the power to forgive.

The idea of sin is not identical with that of moral evil. It is a religious and not an ethical conception and, in the lower stages of religious development, has little connexion with morality. In the complex notion of sin many ideas and emotional attitudes have been combined, some of which go back historically to primitive beliefs in magic and taboo. The Old Testament itself furnishes us with several slightly different thoughts on the nature of sin: that of " uncleanness ", for example, which may be incurred by a man unwittingly; but the central and dominant conception in the Hebrew religion as it came to fulfilment was that of disobedience to God, or what is really the same thing, the breaking of the Covenant. As we have seen, it would be most unjust to allege that for the Hebrew righteousness was nothing but a conformity to the external law. The note of " inwardness " is present in the higher expressions of Jewish piety, and the worshipper may say of the Law not only that it is " out there " to be obeyed, but " thy law is within my heart ". Thus the thought of sin is not simply that of the breaking of a law imposed from above but of a spiritual declension from loyalty, a turning away from God. So the Psalmist prays: " Give me a clean heart, O God, and renew a right spirit within me."

Just as in his teaching on the nature of righteousness Jesus adopts and deepens the noblest insight of Old Testament religion, so in the case of his doctrine of sin we discover nothing which is new in principle. The seat of sin is the heart of man [1] which has ignored

[1] Mark ii. 17.

or turned against the law of God as summed up in the two great Commandments. But this alienation from God and his law is not, it seems, by Jesus attributed solely to the wicked heart of man and his natural selfishness. As we have seen, there is reason to believe that he accepted the current belief that demons were the source of disease, so he speaks of the demons and of Satan as the agents of temptation. In the story of the temptation of the Lord, which must have been recounted by him, unless we suppose that it was a legendary story, the spiritual struggle is not with unworthy suggestions from the inner consciousness but with Satan, who here fills the double rôle of the tester of the righteous, as in Job, and the originator of evil, as in later Jewish belief. That Jesus thought men could be inspired by Satan or dominated by Satan is clear if we take two utterances, both addressed to Peter, as genuine. The first is reported by Mark and Matthew but not by Luke. When Peter " began to rebuke him " after his announcement that the Son of Man must suffer, " he rebuked Peter and said, Get thee behind me, Satan, for thou mindest not the things of God but the things of men ".[1] The second, which is given by Luke only and may be another version of the first placed in a different context, emphasizes the testing function of Satan: " Simon, Simon, behold Satan hath asked to have you (plural, i.e. the Apostles) that he might sift you as wheat." [2] The redeeming work of Jesus, as he conceived it, was, in one of its aspects, the conquest of the powers of evil, the Kingdom of Satan, and his

[1] Mark viii. 33. Matthew xvi. 23. [2] Luke xxii. 31.

victory, or rather perhaps that of the Kingdom of God, is manifested by the cure of disease and also by the remission of sins.

The linking up of sin and disease, however, goes farther than the idea that they both come from the same demonic source. Sin is really like bodily sickness, so much so that Jesus can speak of himself as the physician of souls. "They that are whole have no need of a physician; I came not to call the righteous but sinners to repentance."[1] It may be observed here that the standpoint, superficially so far removed from modern ways of thinking, is really strangely in harmony with our new knowledge of the close relation between the physical, mental and spiritual and with the growing conviction that the work of the physician of the body and that of the pastor of souls cannot be separated from one another without loss on both sides.

The parables which touch on the forgiveness of God are not primarily intended to illustrate the nature of sin, but it is worthy of note that they introduce two pictures of the relation of the sinner to God. He is like a man who has incurred a debt which he cannot pay, or he is "lost" like a sheep or like a son who has left the father's house.

Possibly the question must be asked here whether Jesus taught the doctrine of "original sin". According to the ecclesiastical dogma, the whole of humanity is infected by the taint of sin, and this, not only in that they are prone to evil and actually commit sins, but also in that they are born into the world sinful and guilty, just objects of the wrath of God. The essence

[1] Mark ii. 17.

of the doctrine is stated with masterly succinctness in the opening words of the "Office for the Baptism of Infants": "For as much as all men are conceived and born in sin." This dogma of the Church has been developed from passages in St. Paul's epistles and does not derive directly from the words of Christ.

No hint is to be found in the words of Jesus of the theory that the sin of Adam was the cause of a fall of the whole race. This is, of course, not conclusive evidence that he did not believe it, but it seems to have played no prominent part in his preaching. One of the facts of experience which lie behind the doctrine—that of the apparently universal spread of sin—does seem to be suggested by Christ. The most impressive fact in support of the view that Jesus recognized sinfulness as inherent in humanity is that his prayer, intended for all, includes the petition "forgive us our trespasses", nor can there be any doubt that in his ministry Jesus takes for granted that all men need to repent if they would be ready for the Kingdom. The phrases which verbally suggest the contrary, such as "the righteous who need no repentance", are obviously spoken with bitter irony. To these evidences we may perhaps add the reply to the man who had great possessions: "Why callest thou me good? No one is good, except one, that is God."[1] The need for the penitent attitude is connected with the idea of the service or debt owed to God which even in the case of the most faithful cannot be fully discharged. "When ye shall have done all the things that are commanded you, say, We are

[1] Mark x. 18.

unprofitable servants: we have done that which was our duty to do." [1]

The mission of Jesus then was bound up with the forgiveness or remission of sins. Of that there can be no question; but a problem of great moment arises when we ask, "In what way did Jesus think sins were forgiven and on what conditions?" The doctrine of the atonement has been both a centre of Christian inspiration and a topic of endless controversy, and it is a matter of some delicacy to discuss the words of Jesus which bear upon this subject without offence to the reverence which we rightly feel when approaching in thought the atoning death of Christ. We shall not, we may be sure, greatly err if we sincerely try to discover what, according to our documents, Jesus taught on this matter.

With the possible exception of the author of the Epistle of James, all the New Testament authors believe that the life and death of Jesus, followed by his resurrection, brought into the world a salvation which was not known before and that this salvation means the remission of sins. This belief is clothed in somewhat different forms and worked out on lines which are not always easy to reconcile with one another, but the fundamental agreement on the fact of salvation through Christ is there, plain for all to see. The Gospel of John indicates that the reader is to see in Jesus the cosmic Redeemer at the outset of the book in the "witness of John". "Behold the Lamb of God that taketh away the sin of the world." [2] The coming of the Son who is the word of God, his glorifi-

[1] Luke xvii. 10. [2] John i. 29.

cation in the Passion and his imparting of life to those who eat his body and drink his blood, are the means by which men pass from death to life and from darkness to light. " I am come a light into the world that whosoever believeth on me may not abide in darkness." " This is life eternal that they should know thee the only true God and him whom thou didst send, even Jesus Christ." [1] The rich and various doctrine of St. Paul is developed from one or two leading ideas some of which we have already met in our examination of the teaching of Jesus. The demonic powers have been overthrown by the cross and the new age has begun. The wrath of God against sin has been diverted from the sinner who has faith in Christ, because God has " set forth his Son to be a propitiation or expiation " so that forgiveness can be described as " through faith in his blood "; but further, the believer, in a mystical manner, shares the experience of Christ, being not only " in Christ " but dying and rising with him. The emphasis upon the blood of Christ and the suffering of Christ for others relates St. Paul's doctrine, not only with the sacrifices of the Law, but, more important, with the figure of the Suffering Servant of God in the latter part of Isaiah. The Epistle to the Hebrews presents the fundamental idea of the saving work of Christ in a somewhat different manner by means of an elaborate discussion of the meaning and purpose of sacrifice, with the object of showing that Christ is both the great High Priest and the victim, " Who through the eternal Spirit offered himself unto God ".[2] But the idea of

[1] John xii. 46, xvii. 3. [2] Hebrews ix. 14.

the Covenant is allied with that of sacrifice. Christ has become the Mediator of a new Covenant, and a long quotation of the passage from Jeremiah[1] makes it clear that the author means that the ideal of the martyr prophet has been fulfilled through Christ.

This brief sketch has shown that certain profound religious conceptions, all of which have been derived from the Old Testament, inspired the reflection of the Apostolic Church on the effects of the life and death of Jesus. Chief among them are those of vicarious suffering, symbolized by the Servant of Jehovah, and the New Covenant prophesied by Jeremiah. The problem which has to be considered is, how far were these thoughts or the germs of them already present in the mind of Jesus? Roughly speaking, there are two views on this matter: on the one side are those who hold that the whole of the interpretation of the death of Jesus which we find in the New Testament was the work of the Apostolic Church and that any phrases in the Gospels which attribute such conceptions to Jesus are a reflection of the Church's belief and not of his mind; on the other side are those who hold that the doctrines of St. Paul, Hebrews and St. John, though they are indeed developments, spring from an element in the thought and teaching of Jesus himself. The present writer holds the second opinion, but it is only fair to warn the reader that the subject is controversial and that many eminent scholars hold the first.

We have to admit that one important point must be conceded to those who regard the Pauline doctrine of

[1] Hebrews viii. 8–12, x. 16–17. Jer. xxxi. 31–34.

the atonement as having no root in the mind of Jesus. So far as the Synoptic Gospels tell us, there is no record that Jesus ever said that there was any other means of forgiveness or condition of forgiveness except repentance. The word means "change of mind" and probably stands for an Aramaic word which signifies "turning to God". "A change of mind by turning to God" is as good a description of what Jesus meant by "repentance" as we could find. The teaching on forgiveness is always closely related with the fatherhood of God as is the case in the Lord's Prayer. The Father seeks the sinner and is waiting for him to repent and be forgiven. The parables which most clearly illustrate this are those which are found only in Luke—those of the Prodigal Son and the Pharisee and Publican.[1] In so far as a condition can be said to be laid down other than that of repentance, it is that of readiness to forgive those who have sinned against us. "Whensoever ye stand praying forgive if ye have aught against any one, that your Father also which is in heaven may forgive you your trespasses."[2] The same condition is enforced in the parable of the Unforgiving Debtor, which is given by Matthew in the setting of an answer to Peter's question, How often shall I forgive?[3] But it would be wrong to regard this duty of forgiveness as an additional requirement to that of repentance, for it is really a consequence of genuine turning to God. "If a man say I love God and hateth his brother he is a liar, for he that loveth not his brother whom he hath seen cannot love God

[1] Luke xv. 11–32, xviii. 9–14.
[2] Mark xi. 25.
[3] Matthew xviii. 21–32.

whom he hath not seen." [1] The man who turns to God and loves him at the same time turns to the neighbour with the generous love which forgives "unto seventy times seven".

It might perhaps be argued that the aspect of sin as a debt, which appears in Matthew's version of the Lord's Prayer, and also certain parables, would imply that the debt must be paid by someone and cannot be paid by the sinner. There is, however, no hint of this thought in the words of Jesus. "There is no suggestion of the debt being paid by a third party. It is simply cancelled. Whatever view we may take of the atonement, it must be confessed that the notion of the payment of man's debts to God by Jesus is one which has no support in the teaching of Jesus himself. That teaching is perfectly plain, and it is that the debts are not paid by any one but wiped out by God's grace." [2]

We must on this question agree with Dr. Rashdall when he sums up his discussion by saying: "There is no notion at all that He had brought into the world any new way of procuring forgiveness of sins but this—the way of repentance." [3]

But perhaps this is not the final word. In asserting, as he did assert, that repentance was the requisite for forgiveness and that nothing else was required, Jesus was only repeating what the prophets had said with one voice. No one doubted that if a man could perfectly repent, change his mind by turning to God, he would be answered by complete forgiveness. But the history of the Jews showed that repentance was

[1] 1 John iv. 20. [2] Manson, *Teaching of Jesus*, p. 310.
[3] Rashdall, *Idea of Atonement*, p. 24.

not easy, and that the exhortations of the prophets had not prevented the people of God from falling into the most disastrous evils. In spite of all the prophets, the Kingdom of God had not come, the reign of God in human life had not been established. How was that Kingdom to be brought in with power and the repentant community, " the people of the Saints of the Most High ", to become a reality? When we ask these questions, we can see that the formula " repent and be forgiven " does not cover the whole problem as it certainly does not exhaust the thought of Jesus on the meaning of salvation and the means by which it is procured.

X

THE LAMB OF GOD

AT two decisive moments of his life Jesus spoke words which are mysterious yet highly significant for our understanding of his deepest thought and feeling. As he began his last journey to Jerusalem to die, walking before the amazed and terrified disciples, having predicted his own death and resurrection, he said: "Truly the Son of Man came not to be served but to serve and to give his life a ransom for many."[1] At the Last Supper, on the eve of that predicted death, he took bread and said, "This is my body," and a cup over which he pronounced the words, "This is my blood of the (new) covenant which is shed for many," and he added, "Truly I say unto you, I will no more drink of the fruit of the vine, until that day when I drink it new in the Kingdom of God."[2] Naturally those who are unable to imagine that Jesus could have had any conception of his work and vocation which went beyond those of a rabbi, or entertained ideas which would not commend themselves to a member of a modern Ethical Society, are impelled by their presuppositions to attribute these words to the Christian community and deny that Jesus used them.

[1] Mark x. 45. [2] Mark xiv. 22–25.

But there is no objective reason for rejecting them; they stand in our earliest sources and they are in line with the subsequent belief of the Church. They would explain, what would otherwise be somewhat enigmatic, how the primitive Christian community came to attach atoning and redemptive value to the death of Christ.

The words about the Son of Man giving his life " as a ransom " occur in the immediate context of a dispute as to who should be first in the Kingdom of God, and the primary purpose of the saying is to contrast the principle of the Kingdom with that of the world, but they are clearly also closely connected with the coming suffering and death of Jesus to which he had referred just before. The thought in the mind of Jesus goes back to the Servant of God who suffers, especially to the picture in Isaiah liii. There is reason for believing that Jesus found in this great passage a light on the career and work on which he had embarked. In the predictions of his sufferings echoes of the Servant Songs can be discerned and specially in this saying about the ransom: the word " ransom " itself and the phrase " for many " are reminiscences of the description of God's afflicted Servant—the great exemplar in the Old Testament of one whose glory was service.

The so-called " Servant Songs " in Isaiah are by an unknown author, and the question whether they refer to an historical person, or to an ideal figure, or to the pious remnant of Israel, is one to which no definite answer can be given. Nor does it matter; the point of outstanding importance for the history of religion is that in these chapters sacrifice is taken up into the realm of spiritual reality. The prophet and the priest, often enemies in the development of Hebrew thought, here meet and are reconciled. Those rites of sacrifice, the guilt offerings, which, as the Epistle to the Hebrews tells us, could never take away sin, are now given a prophetic interpretation and seen, as it were, as shadows of a reality only truly known in personal life. " He was despised and rejected of men, a man of sorrows and acquainted with grief . . . he was despised, we esteemed him not (we set him at nought)." " He hath borne our griefs and carried our sorrows. . . . He was wounded for our transgressions, he was bruised for our iniquities, the chastisement of our peace was upon him and with his stripes we are healed. . . . The Lord hath laid on him the iniquity of us all. . . . He bare the sin of many and made intercession for the transgressors." [1]

One of the most inveterate errors of those who interpret religious conceptions and symbols is to translate them into neat summary phrases, which are then analysed as if they were logical propositions. We shall never understand the true significance of any religion, either what it meant for those who through it expressed their feelings and hopes, or its permanent value for the world, if we take for granted that it can be comprehended as a system of " clear and distinct ideas ", or, we may add, if we imagine that truth and reality are wholly capable of being rationalized. To say that the idea in Isaiah liii is that of " vicarious suffering " is to say very little. This poem comes

[1] Isaiah liii.

from the heart of a personal experience of the strange, and indeed rationally inexplicable, power of an utterly unselfish and devoted life. The word which Rudolf Otto uses of the core of this experience, an "irrational element", may be open to question, but what he intends to imply, i.e. that the images used to convey profound emotional change are beyond the scope of logic, is certainly true. "These ideas," he remarks, "have not been thought out at all on the basis of a concept of God, indeed they have not been thought out in any way. Rather they have been born from the experience of sinful men who, by the holy, innocent self-surrender of their master, have experienced a power which atones, washes from impurity, releases from the burden of guilt, heals from spiritual sickness, liberates from error and self-will; and to whom thereby the unapproachable transcendent 'numen' has become a God of the 'berith', the saving Covenant."[1]

That Jesus felt himself to be one with the Suffering Servant of God as well as the Messiah and Son of Man is the clue to the understanding of his most profound words and also of his death. It is clear that he could have avoided the Passion. The last journey to Jerusalem was a challenge to the opposing forces to do their worst, to decide for or against the Kingdom of God, but he knew that the issue would be death and he accepted the will of God as the Servant whose voluntary suffering would be a "ransom for many". The ideas of the Messiah and the Suffering Servant had, so far as we know, never been brought together before. That the Messiah must be rejected, scorned

[1] Otto, *Kingdom of God and Son of Man*, p. 260.

and killed was a thought wholly strange to the Hebrew expectation; he was to be a king, reigning in righteousness and prosperity. Nor again does the Apocalyptic figure of the Son of Man suggest any associations of suffering on behalf of others. He is the supernatural, kingly victor over the powers of evil. Thus Jesus brings together two of the conceptions in which all that was most spiritual and profound in the Hebrew religious experience found its utterance and upon which all its purest emotions centred. But he does this not only in thought but in his own life and consciousness. What we have to contemplate is, not the interesting combination of two concepts never before brought together, but one who was in his own experience both Messiah and Servant and who faced all the consequences.

We must now turn to the words at the Last Supper, bearing these conclusions in mind. The subject is surrounded by controversies which have arisen from the disputes of Christians about the Sacrament of the Eucharist, and every word of the narratives has been a theological battle-ground. We must put these, as far as possible, on one side, not because they are unimportant, but because any discussion of them would obscure the main purpose which we have in this book. What we may hope to do is to discern the chief thoughts and hopes which Jesus expressed at that time; on their application in the life of the Church we will be silent.

We have four accounts of the Last Supper in the New Testament. John, probably on account of his special view of the nature of the Eucharist, has nothing to say of its institution. The earliest, in point of composition, is that given by St. Paul in his first Epistle to the Corinthians,[1] which was called forth by certain disorders and scandals in the Corinthian Church. According to St. Paul, Jesus said: "This is my body which is for you; this do in remembrance of me," and, "This cup is the new Covenant in my blood, this do as oft as ye drink it in remembrance of me." Here we observe that the command to repeat is explicit and there is a definite reference to the new Covenant. St. Paul tells us that he received this "of the Lord" and the phrase has given rise to a doubt whether he means "by revelation" or by tradition. It is impossible to decide this question, but it would appear strange that, if he meant he had obtained his information from Peter or one of the Apostles who were present at the Last Supper, he did not say so. In Mark we read that Jesus said, "Take ye, this is my body." "This is my blood of the Covenant which is shed for many. Verily I say unto you I shall no more drink of the fruit of the vine until that day when I drink it new in the Kingdom of God." [2] Matthew follows Mark closely, except that he adds, after "the blood of the Covenant", "for the remission of sins". The Gospel of Luke, as we have it in the English Bible, has only one serious difference from the other accounts—there are two cups mentioned; but some manuscript authorities give a much shorter text which runs: "And he received a cup, and when he had given thanks he said, Take this and divide it among yourselves, for I say unto you I will not drink

[1] 1 Corinthians xi. 23–25. [2] Mark xiv. 22, 24, 25.

of the fruit of the vine until the Kingdom of God shall come. And he took bread and, when he had given thanks, he brake it and gave it to them saying, This is my body; but behold the hand of him that betrayeth me is with me on the table."[1] A general opinion among scholars prefers this shorter text of Luke as the probable original, since it is easy to see how this might later have been expanded by additions from 1 Corinthians but not easy to see how the longer version could have become contracted.

A comparison of these four stories brings out some interesting facts. Only St. Paul's version includes an explicit command to repeat the ceremony, and it is he alone who definitely represents what happened at the Last Supper as the founding of a sacrament for the Church. No doubt the Evangelists themselves believed that this was what Jesus did, but they do not report words of his to that effect. All the accounts have a reference to the Covenant, or the New Covenant, except the shorter text of Luke.

In view of these facts, we cannot be certain of the precise words which Jesus spoke at the Last Supper, and there is room for much difference of opinion whether St. Paul, Mark or the shorter text of Luke is the most historically accurate. We need not, however, decide this critical question, for the general significance of what was said and done emerges from all the narratives.

The meal of fellowship was not a new thing to the inner circle of the disciples of Jesus; it had no doubt been a frequent and even regular experience during

[1] Luke xxii. 15–22.

the time when they had " continued with him in his temptations ". This one was of peculiar solemnity, not because it was the first, but because it was the last. Meals of fellowship were a common practice among the Jews, quite apart from the Passover meal, and at such repasts it was the custom to pronounce a blessing or a " grace " over a cup of wine or water. The blessing used in the time of Jesus probably included the phrase " the fruit of the vine ", and it is significant that he said at the time when the cup was distributed: " I shall not drink henceforth of the fruit of the vine until the Kingdom of God shall come."

The life of the Kingdom, as we have seen, was very often symbolized by a feast, the Messianic banquet; the idea is frequently found in the parables of Jesus; and the import of the words and acts of Christ here is determined by this realistic image. There will be no more meals of fellowship until the Kingdom of God has come. Jesus makes both a gesture of farewell and a prophecy of future fellowship in the Kingdom; the hour of sadness is the eve of triumph. These two contrasted but related thoughts have always been fundamental in the Eucharist: death and future victory—" we show forth the Lord's death until he come," making a memorial of the Passion and setting it in the light of the future consummation.

The breaking and the distribution of the bread with the words, " this is my body ", are compared by Otto with symbolical actions of the prophets. He cites an interesting parallel from Jeremiah, in which the prophet takes an earthen bottle and breaks it saying: " Thus saith the Lord, even so will I break this people and this city as one breaketh a potter's vessel and it cannot be made whole again."[1] So Jesus breaks the bread as an acted prediction of his death. As the bread is broken so will his body be. The appropriateness of the symbol becomes more complete if we suppose that Jesus expected death by stoning, the appointed penalty for blasphemy.

We may follow Dr. Otto when he proceeds a stage farther in his exposition of the meaning of the broken and eaten bread. He points out that in the Hebrew religious ways of thinking and feeling, as indeed in other religions, the idea of a symbolical action which gives to those who share in it participation in the thing symbolized is not unknown; there is not only representative action but "effective representation", as when the "live coal from the altar" touches the lips of Isaiah and purifies them, imparting to him a consecration for the office of prophet. So Jesus, when he gives the broken bread which represents his body to the disciples, means to include them, to give them participation in, the atoning power of that broken body. This again is an aspect of the Eucharist which has always been preserved: "The bread which we break is it not a communion of the body of Christ?"[2]

Much more no doubt than this most Christians would find in the Last Supper, but what we have discovered to be the minimum significance of the shortest account is sufficiently impressive. The two aspects of Jesus' mission, as he conceived it, are brought together. He is the Messiah and Son of Man, the Kingdom of God has come into the world with him

[1] Jeremiah xix, 11. [2] 1 Corinthians x. 16.

and it will come in power through him; and, at the same time, he is the Suffering Servant of God, who by his voluntary and innocent sacrifice enables many to share in the life of the Kingdom.

But in all the other narrations of the Last Supper, as we have seen, there is a definite reference to the Covenant. Dr. Otto thinks that even Luke has an allusion to the Covenant in the saying, occurring a little later: " I appoint unto you a Kingdom," which he would translate " I covenant unto you." This may be doubtful, but it is at least certain that three out of four of our documents assert that Jesus gave another cup and that he said: " This is my blood of the Covenant," and it may be that, after all, Luke originally said the same. There can be little room for doubt that Jesus spoke of the Covenant in connexion with his death, nor can there be any question that he had in mind the New Covenant of Jeremiah. As we have seen, that great prophetic vision of the time when the Law of God would be written in men's hearts, so that they would no longer need the tablets of stone nor even that one should teach his brother saying, " Know the Lord ", was of all Old Testament scriptures nearest to the mind of Jesus. The whole of his ethical teaching is in line with it. Doubtless it was often in his thoughts and never more clearly than on the eve of the final crisis.

" This is my blood of the New Covenant." It is of quite transcendent importance that these words and their meaning should be kept in mind when we are reflecting on the Last Supper and the last days of Jesus' life. They remind us that, though ideas and emotions are evoked which have their roots far back in history and had even then in some minds superstitious and magical associations, for Jesus they have no such connotation. The Kingdom which he has in mind is not the crude apocalyptic dream of the Book of Enoch, and the efficacy of his death is not that of a cult sacrifice. It is the Kingdom which is based on the New Covenant, the spiritual Covenant; it is still the Kingdom which can be entered only by those who are repenting. The Son of Man gives his life a ransom for many so that they may be able to repent and, in union with him, enter the Kingdom.

According to Mark the only intelligible word which Jesus uttered during the agony of the cross was the cry, "My God, my God, why hast thou forsaken me?" Luke, however, omits this and asserts that Jesus exclaimed, "Father, into thy hands I commit my spirit." Some have found in the dreadful cry "Why hast thou forsaken me?" an indication that the tragedy of the Cross was utterly unrelieved, and that Jesus at his last hour realized the baselessness of the hope upon which he had built. At that moment he abandoned the belief, which he had held until the end, that God would vindicate his Messiah and bring in the Kingdom. In the theology of the Church the moment of "dereliction" has been regarded as the deepest agony of the Passion. It was necessary for the Saviour of the world to taste every bitterness of death, even that, most dreadful of all to him, of being abandoned by God. Neither of these opinions has any secure foundation. As Dr. Rawlinson points out, it is most unlikely that the words would have been preserved in the tradition if they had been understood to be an utterance of despair.[1] In fact the words are the opening line of Psalm xxii, and it is easy to see how naturally that Psalm would come to the mind of Jesus in the time of pain and loneliness. It is the meditation of one who suffers grievous wrong but who clings to faith in the God who "inhabits the praises of Israel". "Thou art he that took me out of the womb; Thou didst make me trust when I was upon my mother's breasts." "Be not thou far off, O Lord; O thou my succour haste to help me." "He hath not despised nor abhorred the affliction of the afflicted, neither hath he hid his face from him."

Our study of the teaching of Jesus has led us to believe that he expected to die and that the suffering of the Son of Man was a necessary prelude to the coming of the Kingdom in power. His words before the Sanhedrin presuppose the conquest of death. According to the Gospels he foretold, on more than one occasion, his resurrection. Many critics dismiss these sayings as additions to the tradition made by the community which was united in the faith of the resurrection, but there is no need to suppose any such thing. It may be that the predictions have, to some extent, been made more definite and explicit than they originally were, but there is every reason to believe that Jesus anticipated his own rising again. He was the Son of Man and also the Suffering Servant of God: to fulfil the destiny of the one he must endure the experience of the other, but the Kingdom in power, the glorious reign of God, must be brought in by the

[1] Rawlinson, *St. Mark*, p. 236.

Son of Man, just as the present Kingdom which was in the world had been brought by him.

The ideas and motives which lie behind the events and words briefly discussed in this chapter belong to a region of thought and experience very remote from many people to-day. It is impossible to treat them as logical counters, nor can they be made plain to those who understand nothing which they cannot define. Theology has sometimes been the enemy of religion because it has attempted the impossible—to exhaust the significance of symbols which stand for deep and indefinable longings, hopes, despairs and triumphs of the spirit in concepts which can be arranged into a neat system. If anyone thinks that Jesus died for a baseless dream he cannot be refuted by logic. To many modern men who have not escaped from the bounds of a narrow rationalism the Cross must appear, as it did to "the Greeks" of old, "foolishness", a sacrifice without intelligible purpose. But no one is a rationalist all the time; and those who have known, in the actual business of living, what it means to be a stranger to reality, out of harmony with the purpose of the world, divided against oneself, have the beginning of an insight into the profound and ineradicable need in man for some deliverance from the self which does not come from within the self. They "have ears to hear" the words "forgiveness" and "redemption". Those who have known, not as an interesting psychological phenomenon but as something lived through, the incalculable power of an utterly devoted life to transform others have the clue to the mystery of the sacrifice of Jesus and its efficacy. No "Strong Son of God" or merely supernatural Son of Man could truly be the Saviour, but only one who loved enough to suffer the utmost. No one can have the least sympathetic grasp of the purpose of Jesus whose hopes are for a political and economic change and nothing more, but only those who know some hint in their own souls of what it means " to hunger and thirst after righteousness ", after the clean heart and the spontaneous goodness which flows from the personality like a fount of living water. But those who have these witnesses in themselves will know and feel that, through the forms which come from the old religion of the Hebrews and are filled with new meaning by Jesus, are revealed eternal realities. In every generation since the Crucifixion " the many " for whom the ransom was given have found in the Cross a power of God unto salvation; they have been made able to repent, to change their minds by turning to God, and have discovered that the New Covenant of the Kingdom was not ancient myth but present fact.

XI

JESUS AND THE CHURCH

THE Christian Church became a separate community at an early date. In the year A.D. 64, as we learn from Nero's persecution of Christians, they were recognized in Rome as distinct from the Jews. But it is clear that at the beginning the difference of the Christians from the rest of the Jewish community did not imply that they thought themselves or were necessarily thought by others to be outside the pale of Judaism. Two closely connected events, or rather processes, led to the historical separation of Christianity from the Jewish religion and fellowship out of which it came. The first was the comparative failure of the Christian propaganda among the Jews. Though it had some success and a Church of definitely Jewish Christians long survived, on the whole both the authorities and the mass of Jews rejected the doctrine that Jesus was the Messiah. The influence of St. Paul was even more decisive. When he turned to the Gentiles he developed those universal and anti-legal elements which were already in the tradition of Christ's teaching and did so in a sharp, antithetical form which precluded any possibility of a reconciliation, for he set aside the law, the distinctive mark of the Jewish Church and race, and insisted that the Christian was not only released from the obligation of the Jewish law but that, if he treated it as still having divine authority, he had fallen away from the "grace which is in Christ Jesus".

Nevertheless there is no thought in primitive Christianity that the Christian was a member of a new community. That with Christ and through his death and resurrection something new had come into the world was indeed the primary conviction of believers; he had brought new life, a new way of approach to God. The Christian felt himself to be a "new creation", but he was nevertheless a part of the old divine society, the holy people. In the prophets there lay ready to hand an idea which might justify the claim to be the true Israel. More than one prophet had declared that only a "remnant" should be saved, and St. Paul seizes upon this prophecy to define the position of the Church. It was the faithful remnant: "even so at this present time also there is a remnant according to the election of grace".[1] Or he goes further and describes the Christians as the true Israel. "They are not all Israel who are of Israel."[2] Israel "after the flesh" is distinguished from the genuine Israel, that after the spirit, which includes all who have faith in Christ, "for neither is circumcision anything nor uncircumcision but a new creation. And as many as walk by this rule peace be upon them and mercy, and upon the Israel of God".[3] Another manner of speaking of the Church which St. Paul uses—as the "body of Christ"—does not conflict with his con-

[1] Romans xi. 5. [2] Romans ix. 6. [3] Galatians vi. 15, 16.

ception of the Church as the true Israel. The Church of the old Law has been transformed by the coming and by the indwelling of Christ through the Spirit, but it is none the less continuous with the ancient holy people.

Thus the question, Did Jesus found the Church? does not represent the New Testament way of looking at the matter. Nobody supposed that the Church was an absolutely new community; it was the fulfilment of Israel; no one supposed that it did not represent that new and final stage in the history of God's revelation which began with the life, death and resurrection of Jesus.

In modern discussions the question whether Jesus founded the Church means, it may be supposed, how far did the Church form a part of the intention and teaching of Jesus? and further, how far did he lay down directions for its life and organization? The second question can receive a summary general answer. We have good reason to believe that he did not make any regulations for the Church, because primitive Christianity appears to have known of none. The development of the organization and worship of the Church is a complex and obscure subject, but we may observe that it seems to have been modelled, as we should expect, from the first on the Synagogue and to have taken different forms, at a later period, in different local Churches. The bitter controversy concerning the admission of the Gentiles to the Church is sufficient to show that there was no authoritative word of the Lord on this vital question known to the contending parties.

The word " Church " is the translation of the Greek word " ecclesia " which itself stands for a common Hebrew word meaning " congregation " or " assembly ". When it occurs in the Gospels, therefore, it need not necessarily be taken to refer to the Christian community. But, in fact, the word appears only twice and in each case in the Gospel of Matthew. In a passage, which begins by referring to the duty of forgiveness, definite rules are laid down about " gaining " the offending brother. If he refuses to hear the injured party the latter is to take witnesses, and if he refuses to hear in these circumstances the saying proceeds, " Tell it unto the church and, if he refuse to hear the church also, let him be unto thee as the Gentile and the publican. Verily I say unto you what things soever ye shall bind on earth shall be bound in heaven and what things soever ye shall loose on earth shall be loosed in heaven ".[1] It seems impossible that these words, as they stand, can represent a genuine saying of Jesus. The passage comes from Matthew's special source and has no support from the other Gospels. The way in which publicans are referred to as equivalent to outcasts conflicts with what we know to have been the actual attitude of Jesus towards this despised class, and, finally, the saying about " binding and loosing " seems to presuppose a state of things in which the Church was so organized as to be able to exercise the power of excommunication. Of course it may be said that Jesus foresaw that time and legislated for it, but the most probable view is that we hear in these words the voice of some section of the early Church.

[1] Matthew xviii. 15–18.

It would be most precarious to base any conclusion about the teaching of Jesus on these verses.

In Matthew's account of the confession of Peter that Jesus is the Messiah he adds some famous and much disputed words. "Blessed art thou, Simon-Bar-Jonah: for flesh and blood hath not revealed it unto thee, but my Father which is in heaven. And I say unto thee that thou art Peter and upon this rock I will build my church, and the gates of Hades shall not prevail against it. I will give unto thee the keys of the Kingdom of Heaven."[1] What these words mean is exceedingly doubtful. Is the "rock" on which the Church will be built, Peter himself, Peter's faith, the belief in the Messiahship of Jesus, or even Jesus himself? Each of these views has been held and for each something can be said. But it is even more doubtful whether the saying is a genuine utterance of the Lord's. There is no trace of anything resembling it in the other Gospels and it is difficult to reconcile with other passages in Matthew itself. How, for example, could the dispute as to who should be greatest among the disciples have arisen, if this emphatic assertion of the primacy of Peter had been in their memories? The one certainty is that the tendency of the passage is to exalt the authority of Peter above that of the other Apostles, and we may conjecture that these verses express the convictions of a circle of Jewish Christians who regarded Peter as their patron and held Paul in suspicion.

The sayings which most explicitly contemplate the existence of the universal Church are those attributed

[1] Matthew xvi. 17–19.

to the risen Christ. "All authority hath been given unto me in heaven and on earth. Go ye therefore and make disciples of all nations, baptizing them into the name of the Father and of the Son and of the Holy Ghost, teaching them to observe all things whatsoever I commanded you, and lo I am with you all the days, even unto the end of the world." [1] "Ye shall receive power when the Holy Ghost is come upon you and ye shall be my witnesses both in Jerusalem and in all Judea and Samaria and unto the uttermost part of the earth." [2] There are difficulties about the first of these sayings which have nothing to do with our belief in the truth of the Resurrection. It is here alone in the New Testament that we have a reference to baptism in the name of the Three Persons; elsewhere we read of "baptism into the name of Jesus" and it is almost certain that this was the primitive custom in the Church. Further, such definite instructions to baptize all nations and to witness to the confines of the world are not easy to harmonize with the reluctance of the Church to launch out into the deep of the Gentile world. But the truth which lies deeper than the details of the reported words of the risen Lord is beyond controversy. It was the belief in the resurrection of the Son of Man which created the Church, first as a distinct sect within Judaism and afterwards, inevitably, as a separate community with a universal mission.

But the Church existed in germ during the ministry of Jesus. The circle of disciples, the "little flock", were the fellowship of those who had accepted the Good News of the Kingdom, and were bound together

[1] Matthew xxviii. 18–20. [2] Acts i. 8.

by a common loyalty to the Lord. Jesus appointed twelve who were called Apostles. The number is significant, for it is plainly intended to correspond with the twelve tribes of Israel. In a strange saying Jesus makes this clear: "Ye shall sit on thrones judging the twelve tribes of Israel".[1] Though Jesus is here evidently thinking of the triumphant Kingdom, the words form a link with the doctrine of the primitive Church that it was the "remnant", the true and spiritual Israel.

Doubtless to some minds it may seem a disappointing result that a candid examination of the evidence leads us to conclude, in the words of Canon Quick, "there is singularly little direct indication that Jesus regarded it as part of his mission to found any religious organization upon earth which would supersede the institutions of Judaism".[2] They would prefer to believe that Jesus laid down the plan of the Church from the beginning and that its ordinances, government and dogmas have been settled by the words of the Lord. But the fact is otherwise, and perhaps a deeper consideration may lead us to see that this freedom from the trammels of a system that cannot be changed is really consonant with the mind of Jesus. He who protested against the letter of the law when it was used to pervert its spirit, and was himself the victim of a rigid and self-confident ecclesiasticism, did not impose upon his disciples a system which might develop all the traits of the Pharisaism with which he was in conflict. The Church is left to the freedom

[1] Luke xxii. 30. Matthew xix. 28.
[2] Quick, *Doctrines of the Creed*, p. 326.

of the Spirit—the most difficult and dangerous of all freedoms and the only one which is worth having. "When he, the Spirit of truth, is come he shall guide you into all the truth."[1] The Church is thrown into the world to be a living organism, adapting itself to the changing environment in which it has to exist, meeting the needs of the times as challenges to new adventures, with the faith that the Spirit of God, which is also the Spirit of Jesus, will not fail. We shall not know what the Church of Christ truly is until it has regained that freedom of the Spirit which St. Paul knew.

[1] John xvi. 13.

XII

JESUS AND HUMAN SOCIETY

AMONG the interpretations of the teaching of Jesus and of the movement which he began must be reckoned the theory that he was a preacher of political and economic regeneration. Friederich Nietzsche saw in the progress of Christianity the triumph of "slave morality" over the heroic type of ideal. In his mouth this was a condemnation of Jesus and his disciples, but others, whose values are different from Nietzsche's, have hailed in primitive Christianity a stirring of revolt among the depressed classes and have even seen in Jesus a proletarian leader. There is nothing to cause surprise in this, for it is only a modern example of an impulse which has been at work ever since the Christian religion ceased to be an obscure sect and became a world force. Men have sought in the words of Jesus authority for the political and social systems which they regarded as good. It would be difficult to name any form of government or social order for which the sanction of Jesus has not been alleged by someone. They range from absolute monarchy through democracy to communism and anarchism. There is at least this to be said on the side of the theory that Christianity was a "proletarian" movement—a large proportion of its adherents in the first century consisted of "small people", of slaves and members of the "working class". St. Paul points this out as an instance of the power of God to use feeble instruments, "For behold your calling, brethren, how that not many wise after the flesh, not many mighty, not many noble are called; but God chose the foolish things of the world, that he might put to shame them that are wise, and God chose the weak things of the world that he might put to shame the things that are strong".[1]

It is nevertheless quite evident that neither Jesus nor primitive Christianity had any conscious or direct relation with social or political revolution. The Apostolic Church was anxious to be on good terms with the Roman authorities and St. Paul regarded the secular power as ordained by God. It is remarkable too that there is no protest in the New Testament against the institution of slavery. The slave who believed was free with the true freedom of the spirit, but he had no encouragement from the leaders of the Church to throw off his earthly bonds. In this attitude of detachment from political and social movements the early Church was following the example of Jesus. It is a singular feature of the teaching of Jesus that, given as it was in a period when the trend of events was plainly moving towards catastrophe, the question which agitated so many minds about the right solution of the problem of obedience to an alien dominion had almost no reflection in his words. That this silence was deliberate cannot be doubted.

[1] I Corinthians i. 26–27.

The one utterance of Jesus which seems to have a political bearing is the famous, "Render unto Cæsar the things that are Cæsar's, and unto God the things that are God's".[1] Enormous structures of political and ecclesiastical theory have been built upon this text, but it may be doubted whether the saying has any general reference to political principles at all. The purpose of the reply is to evade a dilemma. "Certain of the Pharisees and the Herodians" sought to "catch him in talk". Their question, "Is it lawful to give tribute to Cæsar or not?" was well calculated to serve their purpose, for either answer was dangerous. Had Jesus said "no" he would have appeared to range himself with the party of revolt against the Roman government; had he said "yes" he would have seemed to be on the side of the oppressor. He calls for a denarius, the coin which was used to pay the tax, and points out that it bears the "image and superscription" of Cæsar. The point of his reply is that, refusing to answer the general question, he deals with the particular situation. The questioners were enjoying the benefits of civil government under Cæsar, and so long as they did so they had no right to withhold the tribute demanded; the main consideration, however, is that we should render to God what belongs to him. It seems not unlikely that Jesus had in mind the thought that men are made in the image of God, and that the real implication of the saying is, "Give Cæsar these coins, if he demands them; they are in his province; it does not really matter in view of the coming of God's Kingdom, the tribute to which is

[1] Mark xii. 13–17. Luke xx. 20–26. Matthew xxii. 15–22.

not money but repentant persons ". Thus we can deduce no conclusion from these words on the problem of the rights of secular government or its proper nature; they could be consistent with an anarchist theory that government, as such, is evil.

The steady refusal of Jesus to make any pronouncement on political issues was due to the circumstances of the time and the nature of his mission as he conceived it. There was great danger that he would be acclaimed as the Messiah in the popular sense of that word, that he should be regarded as one more of those leaders who, exploiting the messianic hopes of the masses, stirred up revolt and ultimately brought about the war of A.D. 65–70 which wrecked the whole Jewish state. The account of the temptation of Jesus at the outset of his public career clearly retains the memory of a decision made by him before he began his mission, and that decision was to renounce the way of power and therefore of " practical politics ". It was his conviction that the Kingdom of God could not come " with observation ", in the form of a government exercising visible and outward coercion. In order to carry out this programme, adopted from the first, it was necessary to keep strictly aloof from the fierce clash of parties, and any word, even on the most general aspects of political life, would inevitably have involved him in the struggle.

There is, however, another reason. As we have seen, though Jesus was not, as some have thought, dominated by the apocalyptic visions of the coming age in their crude form, we have reason to believe that he expected the coming of the Kingdom in power within a short time. His profoundly original and spiritual conception of the Kingdom had this link at least with the Apocalypses; it would come suddenly and soon and would be brought in by the power of God and not by the contrivance of men. From this standpoint the political and social arrangements of the time were of little importance; they were brief and transitory manifestations of a world partly in the dominion of evil spirits, which would vanish in the glorious Kingdom of the Son of Man. It is therefore in vain that we scan the records for directions or suggestions immediately relating to our political, social and economic problems, and those who claim Jesus for a party or a theory are reading their own desires and hopes into the Gospels. It does not follow from this that the teaching of Jesus is quite irrelevant to the question, What is the ideal society? To the implications of his doctrine for social ideals we must briefly return.

But before we proceed with this subject we must notice what Jesus has to say on that other human institution—the family. The words of Jesus on this subject have, at first sight, a contradictory appearance, which turns out on examination to be illusory. The life of the family for Jesus was the normal and proper life of man. The relation of father to child is the symbol, or rather sacrament, of the relation of God to man, and the qualities which are required of those who would be able to "accept" the Kingdom of God, or to "enter" it, are illustrated by a little child. Nor again does Jesus question the Jewish belief that the family is more than a human institution; it is of divine origin and has the sanction and blessing of

God. He refers to the original purpose of marriage as a sacred thing when he discusses the Mosaic laws of divorce. The question for him is not one of convenience or expediency or even social welfare but of obeying the will of God.

The teaching of Jesus on divorce, which has been so hotly debated, is, in the main, perfectly clear. The occasion appears to have been one of the numerous attempts to involve him in some embarrassing dispute; this time the controversy between two different schools of Jewish thought on the subject of divorce. The one (Hillel was the representative Rabbi) interpreted the Law in such a manner as to make divorce very easy for the man, even on what appear to us quite trivial grounds; the other (of which Shammai was the spokesman) allowed divorce for no cause except the adultery of the woman. Divorce of the husband by the wife was not allowed by the Jewish Law, though it was in the Roman empire. Jesus replies by asking what the Law of Moses actually said, on which the questioners refer to the regulation in Deuteronomy about a "bill of divorcement". Jesus thereupon states his own principle. "For your hardness of heart he wrote you this commandment. But from the beginning of the creation male and female made he them. For this cause shall a man leave his father and mother, and shall cleave to his wife, and the twain shall become one flesh, so that they are no more twain but one flesh. What therefore God hath joined together let not man put asunder."[1] Matthew adds the clause "except for adultery", which would make Jesus agree with

[1] Mark x. 2–12.

Shammai. There is little doubt that Mark gives the original saying more closely and that Matthew's addition is due to the practical difficulty found quite early by the Church in applying the principle of indissoluble marriage as a law. It should be observed that, here as elsewhere, Jesus appeals to the spirit and intention of the law against its letter. He does not reject the Mosaic regulation as worthless; but he regards it as representing a state of things far below the ideal. It was for the " hardness of heart " of men. The ideal of marriage is stated in the creation story when God made Eve for Adam. " He appeals behind the Mosaic toleration and regulation of divorce to the primary institution of marriage as such, and deduces from Genesis the ideal of permanent and indissoluble marriage."[1] The verses which follow in Mark report a brief conversation " in the house ", in which Jesus is reported to have underlined the public utterance by adding that a man who puts away his wife and marries another commits adultery and that the same is true when a woman divorces her husband. The reference to the case of the wife divorcing the husband is puzzling if the practice was unknown among the Jews, and it may be that the whole of the explanation " in the house " is really comment by the Evangelist, who was writing for Gentile Christians. In view of the whole passage it seems impossible to doubt that Jesus asserted an ideal of marriage which went beyond the stricter school of the Rabbis and treated it as indissoluble. On the other hand, there is no ground for supposing that he intended his words to be re-

[1] Rawlinson, *St. Mark*, p. 134.

garded as a law or that they should be necessarily embodied in civil legislation.

While, however, Jesus places a high value on the life of the family and takes a stricter view of the obligations of marriage than the most rigid of the Jewish parties, there are sayings, some of them startling in their emphasis, which restrict the scope of the family loyalty. Evidently he believed it to be an institution which belonged to the present age and not to the Age to Come. In the triumphant Kingdom of God the marriage relation does not exist. "When they shall rise from the dead they neither marry nor are given in marriage, but are as the angels in heaven." [1] The reason for this is doubtless, as Dr. Rawlinson points out, that where death is abolished the need for birth and for marriage to continue the race no longer exists,[2] but probably Dr. E. F. Scott is right when he sees a further and deeper cause in the conception which Jesus had of the nature of the Kingdom. "He believed that when the will of God was established everywhere there could be no place for anything that made for separation. All souls would depend immediately on God, all interests would be directed to the one goal of serving Him." [3]

Jesus himself places definite limits on the obligation to the family in his own conduct. The mother and brethren of Jesus appear to have been alarmed at his prominence and their visit to him early in his ministry was probably with the purpose of prevailing upon him to

[1] Mark xii. 25. Matthew xxii. 30. Luke xx. 35.
[2] Rawlinson, *St. Mark*, p. 168.
[3] E. F. Scott, *Ethical Teaching of Jesus*, p. 96.

abandon it. We are given the impression from the narrative that he refused to see them and thereupon proclaimed his independence of the family in memorable words: "Who is my mother and my brethren? And looking round on them that sat round about him he saith, Behold my mother and my brethren! For whosoever shall do the will of God, the same is my brother and sister and mother." [1] Nor was this attitude towards loyalty to the family one which he deemed proper to himself alone as the Messiah, for he demands in his disciples a drastic detachment from what are normally regarded as family duties. To one who asks to be allowed to bury his father he replies, "Follow me and leave the dead to bury their own dead". The following of Jesus means leaving father, mother, sisters and brothers. According to Luke Jesus said to the crowd which went with him, "If any man cometh unto me and hateth not his own father and mother and wife and children and brethren and sisters, yea and his own life also, he cannot be my disciple".[2] It is true that in Matthew's version of the saying we have simply the assertion that a disciple must love Jesus more than he loves his family, but there can be no doubt that he used vehement language on the necessity of putting the claims of the family in the second place when they were in conflict with those of the Kingdom of God. Implied in this assertion of the supremacy of the Kingdom is, of course, a moral judgment of a far-reaching character. The family, though a divine institution and an essential condition of human welfare,

[1] Mark iii. 31–35. Matthew xii. 46–56. Luke viii. 19–21.
[2] Luke xiv. 26.

might become an obstacle to the true life of the individual; family affection might be an enlarged and refined selfishness, and family loyalty a hindrance to the larger loyalty of the Kingdom.

We have seen that any pretence to base a political, economic, or social theory on the words of Jesus is due to misunderstanding, but it would be equally misleading to conclude that his teaching has no social implications. Certain ideas which he expressed have worked like leaven in the soul of Christendom and are still working. Jesus stands at the opposite pole to those ancient philosophers who regarded the city or the state as of higher worth than the persons who compose it. There is no word of his which would justify such a conception, still less one which would suggest approval of the modern worship of the state. Implicit in all Jesus' teaching is the supreme value of the individual. As the Father's representative, he seeks them one by one, and his thought of the love of the Father for men is not that of a general benevolence towards the human race but rather of a particularized love, which is directed towards each human being in his own unique circumstances and character. The Church was true to the mind of Christ when it pictured him as the Good Shepherd who " calls his sheep by name " and insisted on the infinite worth of every person as a " brother for whom Christ died ". The consequences of this standpoint, when translated into social action, cannot be other than revolutionary. Any one who accepts the teaching of Jesus is bound to condemn every state of society which does not permit the free expansion and expression of all persons. From

Christian roots the ideal of liberty, equality and fraternity has sprung, though the political interpretation of the ideal has been very far from the spirit of Jesus. Liberty, so we read his thought, can be the possession only of one who has achieved inner freedom by repentance and turning to God; equality is not true on the empirical plane, where we reckon men's various capacities and characters, but only on the plane of religious faith, where we consider each man as the potential child of God; fraternity is a vain dream, unless it be the natural and spontaneous fruit of the faith in the universal fatherhood of God.

If we were compelled to answer the question, What kind of human social order would be nearest to the ideal of Jesus? we should have to set on one side those projects for Utopia which find salvation for mankind in a reign of law or in the creation of a highly efficient state—even though it were a world state. The rule of law is indeed a necessary stage in the progress of mankind, and we can find no word of Jesus which would encourage one to resist the development towards a civilization united under one government, but we should be far from the truth if we imagined that such a condition of things was even the beginning of the Kingdom of God. From the standpoint of Jesus, all laws and regulations which depend upon the sanction of force, or even on the acknowledged expediency of authority, are temporary accommodations to the imperfection of humanity; they are "for the hardness of men's hearts". The social ideal which emerges from a contact with the mind of Jesus might perhaps be described as "the higher anarchism"—

that of a society which no longer needs the constraint of rule and legality, because it is the fellowship of persons who have "the law in their hearts" and, having passed beyond the sphere of "claims and counter-claims", are living together "like dear children" in the family of God. That anything more than a faint approximation to this is impossible on this earth and in the circumstances of human life may well be true, but the vision haunts our imagination like the memory of a home from which we have been long parted.

INDEX